A COMING OF WIZARDS
A MANUAL OF HUMAN POTENTIAL

Michael E. Reynolds

©COPYRIGHT 1989
by High Mesa Press
ISBN 0-9614010-3-6

First Printing: September 1989

Design
Illustration
Photography
by
Michael Reynolds

with help from
Chris
Justin
Tanya
Jonah
Peter

THE HIGH MESA FOUNDATION
P.O. Box 2267
Taos, New Mexico 87571

This book has been printed on partially recycled paper.

This book centers around and was inspired by an experience with four wizards. From this experience I have developed a way of thinking and living that is vividly expressed in my architectural work. I wrote this book to present both the method of thinking and the architectural work, as together they are taking me on a journey I feel would be valuable to document.

The book can be thought of as having three parts. Part one calls forth an appropriate state of mind from which to perceive the "Wizard Information." The journey begins here with the human condition, and slowly moves out of it as the book progresses.

Part two presents the "Wizard Information" along with a real and existing way of applying it in our reality. This is where my architectural work appears- as an example of this type of thinking manifesting a new reality.

The third part moves beyond our own reality, via the "Wizard Information," into the universe and toward an image of God.

Thus, the book is a journey toward a state of mind from which the "Wizard Information" can be perceived. It then moves through that information and beyond the human condition. It is about finding and moving toward our potential. My hope is that opening this book to any page will present some aspect of this potential.

Thank you for your attention,

Michael E. Reynolds

CONTENTS

PREFACE

Immediately after graduating from architecture school in 1969, I moved to Taos, New Mexico, because I had been there on vacation and loved it. Taos is a Spanish/ Indian/ Anglo valley flanked on the northeast by beautiful mountains including the sacred mountain of the Pueblo Indians. This mountain is said to be one of the power spots on the planet. To the southwest of Taos lie rolling mesas covered with sage and cactus, cut sharply by the Rio Grande Gorge and extending on into the sunset and the ever more distant mountains.

Since I moved here I have never wanted to leave. Something happened to me here. I felt so at home that I think I must have stumbled onto my own energy. What I mean is, I found that particular state of mind which allows the oneness or wholeness of the universe to prevail over human dogma. I believe this state of mind is a key to the limit-less energy of the universe.

This realization may have been enhanced by the research I had been doing with pyramids. Both historical and scientific research in this realm lead me to believe that matter appropriately aligned and proportioned in the pyramid shape allows an intensi-fied contact with the energy of the universe at large.

I became so enthralled with pyramids that I built a large, perfectly scaled one on top of my house and had my bed right at the king's chamber location. So here I was, sleeping in a pyramid in a beautiful valley at the base of a sacred power mountain, in a land so akin to the very essence of my own being that it felt like it ran in my body, through my veins and out again.

My work as an architect/builder began to reflect what was happening to me. The earth became a sacred place that I wanted human life to embrace rather than exploit. I set about trying to achieve this for myself and others. I became focused on developing self-sufficient housing made from recycled materials using energy from the sun and wind.

During this time, in the early 1970's, I began having intense experiences, dreams, in-stances of automatic writing, and out-right visions. The highlight came one afternoon when I was lying up in the pyramid on my back just gazing into space. I was not on any drug, alcohol or other mind altering substance. In this relaxed, open state of mind enhanced by the pyramid, I was visited in a vision by four wizards. They clearly and vividly made me aware of a way of seeing and moving that grows in potential through use, with apparently infinite resonance.

I gave cautious consideration to this at first, but then as I began to find similarities between their information, eastern mysticism and quantum physics (which are currently finding similarities to each other) along with traditional religion, the ways of the Shaman, the nature of plants and animals, and the processes of the planet itself, I became less cautious and more focused about this information. I found myself on a journey to a world that reflects more than just the human condition.

This book is my documentation of that journey. In the appendix are a few unedited excerpts from a journal I was keeping at the time. They are included to frame the state of mind from which I pursued my work, lived my life and wrote this book.

Because this book is based on a journal, it is simply a telling of what I have seen. In order to communicate this in terms acceptable to our reality, I have related certain aspects of the text to currently existing realms of thought such as quantum physics, astro-physics, religion, psychology, ecology, and nature in general. I have also used such currently accepted methods of communication as language, mathematics, and graphics.

All of the above realms of thought and methods of communication have limits because they are all conceived by and for the human condition. However, if one wishes to communicate something to others, one must relate in terms that those others are open to. Unfortunately, the power we give existing realms of thought and methods of communication (our collective dogma) tends to limit our ability to see anything in any terms other than that existing dogma.

This dilemma has limited our ability to include, for example, the relatively new found world of quantum physics in our daily reality. Quantum physics is the study of the world inside the atom, the nature of the various particles and forces of which the atom is composed. Particles of matter are so minute here that matter itself appears to be simply energy and energy potentially matter. Inside the atom we have a void of potentiality much like the void spoken of in mysticism. Much has been written in the last decade about the similarities and parallels between quantum physics and mysticism. These works seem to be pushing the little understood quantum reality into the less understood spiritual reality. Thus we are beginning to have a loosely lumped "catch-all" category of phenomenon and realms we do not understand under the vague heading called God.

Throughout history, humans have established a pattern of calling phenomenon that is not understood, God. We have had fire gods, sun gods, rain gods, thunder gods, earth gods, and plant gods. As we grew to understand these phenomenon, we moved the title God on out to the realms that we still did not understand thus keeping God always just out of reach and ourselves always reaching. Now we have found a reality in the subatomic world of quantum physics that we cannot understand, and we find ourselves calling photons and electrons, God.

Our efforts to define God when we do not know exactly what we are, seem to be premature if not ridiculous. The Bible says humans were created in the image of God. If this is the case, we would need simply to find *ourselves* to have the potential to know the image of God. Only then could we even begin to be in a position to entertain the thought of what God actually is; and then I suspect it will not matter.

I am more taken
    by one who lives the truth
    than by one who speaks it.

CHAPTER ONE
LOOKING AT
THE HUMAN CONDITION

Humanity

The Bible says that Humanity was simply "created" in the "image of God." Science says that Humanity "evolved" from tiny organic creatures in the early waters of the planet-gasses sparked into organic life by lightning and/or cosmic rays. (Laboratory simulation experiments have been done to verify this is possible). Both the Bible and science can be right. Humanity could have been created in the image of God via evolution. The questions here are:

What is meant by the image of God?
and
What *exactly* is evolution?

Both of these questions are addressed throughout this book.

According to the theory of evolution, tiny water creatures first learned how to reproduce themselves and then evolved into water creatures with appendages (fins). Over thousands of years some of them ventured to the shallow edges of the water and eventually their fins evolved into feet and they left the water. They had actually become "water with feet" as the bodies of these creatures were mostly water themselves.

Evolution, while not thoroughly understood, is a tangible force, visible even in our own bodies. An example we can relate to is a callus. First we get blisters, and in response to them, our bodies produce a callus where the blister had been. The callus is a tougher form of skin manufactured by the body in response to excessive wear in a specific area. Out bodies adapt/evolve.

Some of the creatures that left those early waters evolved into mammals and others into reptiles. Over eons, some of the mammals evolved larger brains with more neurons to aid their unconscious evolution with consciousness. The mammals who found consciousness and awareness, gained "control" of the planet and we call them human.

Water creatures, through development of their legs, left their water home, their womb, their "reality"- a major leap, a transformation. Likewise, humans through exploration and acquaintance with consciousness, can leave home, womb, and reality. How far will we be able to go? How far do we want to go? We have not begun to realize the potential of this thing called consciousness in the human condition. Will consciousness reveal itself as an entity without need of a body? Are there more major leaps and transformations ahead?

To look at the above questions requires venturing outside the limits of our present reality. In order to "break out" of a reality (in our case, the human condition) we must thoroughly examine it. This is similar to prisoners examining plans of their prison before they break out. They are looking for the place to make a break. The "prison" the human condition finds itself in is strong. One must search for places to make a break. One such place is consciousness itself. The journey begins here.

Consciousness

Consciousness is not a result of the human body and it's brain. Actually, it is quite the opposite. The human body and its brain are results of consciousness. Just as the "force" of gravity on the water going down your bathtub drain creates a vortex or whirlpool, the "force" of consciousness on energy creates what we call "life", the human body and its brain. The whirlpool is but one of many forms that water takes in response to gravity. We are but one of many forms that energy takes in response to consciousness.

Just as gravity is the continuous, self-organizing force particular to all matter- not just water; consciousness is the continuous, self-organizing force particular to all energy- not just us. Consciousness is greater than we are. Consciousness is not a part of us, rather we are a part of consciousness. If consciousness was a part of us, it would be subject to our limitations. If we accept the fact we are a part of consciousness, we have available to us "zones" beyond simple human consciousness where limitation is not a relevant concept. Thus the stage is set to journey beyond the human condition.

While gravity appears to be somewhat more tangible than consciousness, it is just as illusive when we try to pinpoint what it actually is. We know that matter is organized via gravity and the collective view of modern physics and eastern mysticism is beginning to suggest that energy truly is "organized" via consciousness. This being the case; since energy can be converted to matter and matter to energy ($E=MC^2$), we have a profound relationship between gravity and consciousness. Matter and energy *are* the universe; gravity and consciousness *organize* it. The greater the mass, the greater the gravity. The greater the energy, the greater the consciousness. There is always a greater gravity. The moon is in the gravitional field of the earth; the earth gravitates around the sun; the sun feels the gravitational pull of the Milky Way Galaxy; etc. So it is there is always a greater consciousness:

Human consciousness:
Awareness of the individual. The "me". The ego.
The Self.
Unfortunately, we seem to dwell here.

Life consciousness:
The Self as a integral part of all that lives. The "us". All life on the planet. We can project ourselves here but we can't dwell here until we have expanded to include this realm into our selfness- that is, until our human consciousness will admit it is but a part of life consciousness.

Angel consciousness:
All that is. This includes life consciousness, human consciousness and all "nonliving" matter, forces, elements etc. On a limited basis, we can project ourselves toward this condition but we are just beginning to understand it enough to allow that projection. Sometimes if we surrender, our human consciousness will drift out (without a map) but our ego gravity most always pulls us back. It seems we must *break out* of one aspect of consciousness to move to another, much the same way we have to *break out* of the earth's gravity to physically go to another heavenly body.

This "breakout" can be related to a butterfly breaking out of one stage of development (a caterpillar in a cocoon) into another stage, the butterfly itself. The human brain is very much like a caterpillar in a cocoon. The cocoon in this case is the human body. The caterpillar, which is an *aspect* of the butterfly, becomes the butterfly. The brain which is an *aspect* of consciousness, can become consciousness.

4

THE ENERGY BAND

DOGMA AND EGO CREATE A "GRAVITY" THAT DELAYS OUR TRANSFORMATION INTO CONSCIOUSNESS. CONSEQUENTLY OUR COCOON (BODY) OFTEN DIES BEFORE TRANS-FORMATION TAKES PLACE. NATURE MOVES THE CATERPILLAR IN A NATURAL "CURRENT," WHICH IS UNHAMPERED BY DOGMA AND EGO, TO THE STAGE OF BUTTERFLY. NATURE HAS A NATURAL CURRENT FOR US TOO. THIS CURRENT IS A BAND OF ENERGY THAT WILL MOVE US TO OUR OWN POTENTIAL- OUR BUTTERFLY FORM- **PURE CONSCIOUSNESS.**

THIS BAND OF ENERGY IS LIKE THE STRONG CURRENT IN THE MIDDLE OF A RIVER. THERE ARE MANY EDDIES AND PLACES ON EITHER SIDE OF THE MIDDLE WHERE THE CURRENT IS NONEXISTANT OR NOT AS STRONG. THESE EDDIES ARE LIKE DOGMA AND EGO- THEY KEEP US FROM BEING IMMERSED IN THE CURRENT. WE HAVE THE CHOICE IN LIFE TO FIND AND BE CARRIED BY THIS STRONG CURRENT. WE HAVE THE CHOICE TO ALIGN WITH AND SURRENDER TO OUR ENERGY BAND.

BRAIN RESEARCH CONFIRMS THERE IS EASILY AS MUCH DIFFERENCE BETWEEN OUR "PRESENT BRAIN" AND ITS POTENTIAL, AS THERE IS BETWEEN A CATERPILLAR AND A BUTTERFLY. THE BRAIN IS FED MATTER (SUBSTANCES IN THE BLOOD STREAM) THAT IT CONVERTS INTO EVERGY. IF WE ALLOW THIS ENERGY TO FLOW IN OUR ENERGY BAND, IT CAN SPARK GREATER CONSCIOUSNESS LIKE LIGHTNING SPARKED ORGANIC LIFE FORMS IN THE EARLY GASES OF THE EARTH. HOWEVER, WE USUALLY CHOOSE TO USE THIS ENERGY FOR DEVELOPING A "GREATER CATERPILLAR" IN-STEAD OF ALLOWING NATURE TO USE THIS ENERGY FOR DEVELOPING A "BUTTERFLY." THIS KEEPS US OUT OF THE STRONG CURRENT OF OUR ENERGY BAND AND TRAPPED IN AN "EDDY."

IF WE CHOOSE TRANSFORMATION RATHER THAN DEVELOPMENT OF A "GREATER CATERPILLAR", WE ACCEPT THE FACT THAT TRANSFORMATION IS A FUNCTION OF THE FOLLOWING THREE THINGS: A HEALTHY BODY FOR FEEDING THE BRAIN, ENERGY PRODUCED BY THE BRAIN, AND SURRENDER OF THIS ENERGY TO ONES OWN NATURAL ENERGY BAND.

WE CAN BRING FORTH FIRE FROM TWO STICKS OR A MATCH, BUT FIRE LATENTLY EXISTS IN THE UIVERSE REGARDLESS OF US. LIKEWISE, WE CAN BRING FORTH GREATER CONSCIOUSNESS WITH OUR BRAIN BUT CONSCIOUSNESS EXISTS IN THE UNIVERSE RE-GARDLESS OF US. THE PROPER USE OF A MATCH IS TO STRIKE IT- FIRE COMES. THE PROPER USE OF OUR BRAIN IS TO FIND AND CHANNEL ENERGY TO OUR ENER-GY BAND- GREATER CONSCIOUS-NESS COMES. THIS "FINDING" WILL NOT BE A DISCOVERY OR AN ACHIEVEMENT- RATHER IT WILL BE AN ALIGNMENT AND A SURRENDER.

The human being can surrender to
    greater consciousness just as a
    caterpillar surrenders to a
    butterfly.

The energy band is the natural
    evolutionary "current" that
    energizes these transformations.

Surrender to what you are
    and become it.

This will lead you to your energy band.

When you find your energy band
    there will be no more barriers.

I was walking on the mesa at night
from Beth's house to mine.

There is a thin path to follow
that winds through the cactus and the sage.

It was dark- there was no moon.

I knew the path was there but I could not see it.

I felt the path but if I looked for it I could not see it.

It was too dark.

If I didn't look too hard but just kind of glanced down,
the faint glimmer of the path would
glow through the darkness and guide me.

If I looked hard for it,
for its definition, it would disappear.

Thus is the path of the energy band.

A DRINKING GLASS IS HELD UPSIDE DOWN AND PRESSED FLAT INTO A PAN OF WATER (1&2). THE LEVEL OF THE WATER DOES NOT COME UP INTO THE GLASS BECAUSE THE GLASS IS FULL OF AIR. HOWEVER, IF THE GLASS IS TILTED SIDEWAYS, SOME OF THE AIR ESCAPES AND WATER TAKES THE PLACE OF THE AIR (3). IF THE GLASS IS THEN PULLED UP VERTICALLY SO THE MOUTH OF THE GLASS IS ONLY SLIGHTLY BELOW THE SURFACE OF THE WATER, THE LEVEL OF THE WATER IN THE GLASS WILL BE HIGHER THAN THE LEVEL OF THE WATER IN THE PAN (4). THIS HAPPENS BECAUSE ONCE THE AIR HAS LEFT, SOMETHING HAS TO TAKE ITS PLACE. IN OUR ATMOSPHERE THERE CANNOT BE A VACUUM. A GLASS FULL OF AIR WILL NOT ALLOW WATER TO ENTER (2) BUT IF THE AIR IS LET OUT, WATER WILL CLIMB UP INTO THE GLASS (4).

MIND SPACE
THERE IS AN ELEMENTARY SCHOOL EXPERIMENT USED TO ILLUSTRATE THAT AIR TAKES UP SPACE.

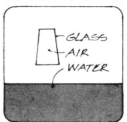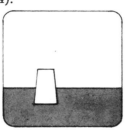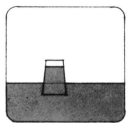

OUR HUMAN "MIND SPACE" IS LIKE THE GLASS IN FIG. 2. IT IS FULL- FULL OF DOGMA, DEFINITIONS AND IMAGES. THE WATER IN THIS EXAMPLE IS ANALOGOUS TO THE "SEA OF ENERGY" AROUND US, WHICH CAN ENTER INTO US VIA OUR ENERGY BAND IN THE FORM OF FEELINGS SUCH AS INTUITION, IMAGINATION, AND INSPIRATION. THESE FEELINGS ARE ASPECTS OF OUR ENERGY BAND. WE DO NOT HAVE ROOM FOR THEM IN OUR MIND SPACE BECAUSE OUR MIND SPACE, LIKE THE GLASS, IS FULL.

MAKING MIND SPACE IS SIMPLY A WAY OF OPENING OURSELVES TO SOMETHING BESIDES WHAT WE FEED BACK TO OURSELVES. THIS ENRICHES OUR LIVES WITH AN OUTSIDE INGREDIENT; THAT IS, AN INGREDIENT OUTSIDE OUR PRESENT REALITY. AS IT IS, OUR REALITY RECYCLES OUR ENERGY BACK INTO ITSELF AND GAINS AN INCREASINGLY INTENSE AMOUNT OF GRAITY TO HOLD AND MOLD US. THIS RESULTS IN AN *INTROVERTED EVOLUTION*. THUS WE BECOME MORE DEVELOPED CATER-PILLARS BUT NEVER MAKE THE LEAP INTO BEING BUTTERFLIES. WE BECOME AN ISOLATED RESULT OF OUR REALITY- SOMETHING LIKE INBREEDING. WE SHOULD NOT BE A RESULT OF OUR REALITY. OUR REALITY SHOULD BE A RESULT OF US.

Mind space can be of infinite proportions or as tiny as a single human ego.

8

Mind space allows a thing we call
  enlightenment

Enlightenment does not have to be
  so aggressively sought after

Enlightenment is simply there in our genes
  and in the cosmos at large

All we have to do is make space for it.

THE INTUITIVE VOICE
THERE IS A VOICE INSIDE

IT SCREAMS IN ANGUISH WHEN
THE POISON OF MALICE FLOWS

IT SINGS WHEN WE GIVE
IT SHUDDERS WHEN WE RECEIVE

IT CRIES WHEN WE ARE FAR FROM
THE ENERGY BAND

IT CALLS ON CURIOSITY AND
EXCITEMENT TO MAKE
ADRENALIN FLOW AND MAGNIFY
LIFE WITHIN

IT MOANS WHEN WE RESIST
OR ARGUE

IT CHOKES WHEN DOGMA FILLS
OUR MINDS AND HOLDS US
EARTH-BOUND

IT IS FAINT BUT WITH UNYIELDING
PERSISTANCE IT EXISTS

OFTEN TO BE IGNORED
OR LAUGHED AT

HEAR THIS VOICE
TRUST THIS VOICE
FOLLOW THIS VOICE
AND YOU WILL RISE ABOVE THE
        EARTH.

Images and Form

Existing dogma and collective ego harness us with introverted thought patterns that dictate definitions of ourselves and our reality. The images resulting from these thought patterns form barriers that block and delay the natural flow of our energy band. A "no image" state (mind space) allows an uninhibited flow of energy that reaches us via what we call "feelings" (intuition, imagination, inspiration). These feelings are then interpreted by logic. Logic (a human phenomenon) is an immediate reaction to outside stimuli, perceived through the senses and received by the brain. Intuition, imagination and inspiration are the lights that illuminate logic. Logic is a phenomenon isolated to our own reality while energy (what we register as feelings) is universal. Logic thus needs an "open channel" with this energy to communicate with the universe. *The energy band is the open channel for this communication.* Images inhibit this communication and in some cases block it altogether.

Beyond the dense foliage of logic. . . lies the clearing of intuition.

The power of images is great as it relates to and directs the attitudes of the "swarm" of humanity. Individuals within the swarm relate to images of human life style, male-female images, religious images, astrological images, political images, etc. These images provide the security within the swarm. The security of the swarm is the root of its power as it ruthlessly stymies and controls energy within its own introverted evolution. The human need and desire (addiction) for the security provided by the images of the swarm is the chain that anchors humans to their particular dimension in a universe of infinite dimensions. *Security is simply a poor substitute for awareness.*

Humanity is a creature seeking security from itself. Beyond insecurity there is flight.

Images are the language of our human condition. They are the "meat" of our reality. They are, however, non-transportable. Our images and forms have no significance outside the human condition. If one is to explore beyond the human condition, one must understand *our attachment to images is one of the reasons we rarely it.*

When we experience dreams, visions, and even drug induced altered states, we notice that our familiar images do not follow the same rules they do in what we call reality. This should give us a clue as to the inadequacy of images in these realms. Logic deals in images. Therefore, we cannot take logic outside our human condition. Feelings deal in energy. Energy can move from outside the human condition into the human condition via feelings. These feelings will eventually manifest images and forms in the human condition. It is these feelings that are the seeds of the form of our reality. We then define a dogma for this form and become attached to it. This is like picking a blossom or flower off a plant. We have interrupted the process, broken the cycle. The flower will soon die. Likewise we tend to isolate form from its ever-evolving cycle, thus from its relationship to energy. So we have isolated ourselves from the energy band. We end up with crystalized images and forms that are not capable of change, of evolution, of growth of movement.

OUR CRYSTALIZED FORMS AND IMAGES HAVE INTROVERTEDLY EVOLVED INTO MASSIVE ENTITIES WHICH NOT ONLY RUTHLESSLY MANIPULATE US; THEY ARE ACTUALLY BEGINNING TO CONSUME US AND OUR PLANET. THEY ARE CALLED CITIES- DRAGONS THAT CONSUME MIND SPACE AND FOSSEL FUEL. OUR CURRENT LIFE PROCESS KEEPS FEEDING HUMAN BEINGS TO THE DRAGONS. THOSE ON WHOM THE DRAGONS CHOKE WILL NOT BE CONSUMED. THEY WILL EVOLVE BEYOND THE DRAGON.

I often walk out on the mesa
    through the sage, the cactus and the onion grass

If I walk in the same direction over and over again, I create a path
    that gets easier and easier to see and follow, for myself and others.
This path becomes a reality and *remains* a reality for a long time
    even though I may never walk on it again.

The same is true for the "paths" we take and have taken
    collectively and individually with our beingness - our energy.

Our "paths" become and remain realities.
The path we create today we will reckon with tomorrow.

Sustenance and Essense

The forms, images, and paths we have created are but expressions of energy that moved into the human condition via feelings. They are the product of feelings. This product crystalizes without an unbroken link with the energy that "inspired" it. Thus the energy band is imperative to the processes of evolution. There is only so far we can go as caterpillars. This is why the physical expressions of our way of life, our cities, have become ruthless dragons. For us to "choke the dragons," we must maintain our link with our energy band.

In terms which are more tangible relative to the human condition, we must maintain a way of life where sustenance, that which sustains us, is aligned with essence, that which *is* us.

For example, we have at least three realms of beingness. We have bodies, minds and spirits. In our current reality we have "jobs" that sustain our existence. Most often these jobs do not sustain or nurture our bodies, minds and spirits. They just sustain a crystalized image of existence. We have to go to spas for our bodies, various entertainment centers for our minds and religious institutions for our spirits. These, at best, only provide a token of what our three realms of beingness really long for. Our daily "work" (our sustenance) is most often not aligned with the daily needs of body, mind and spirit (our essence).

Thus, we have produced a condition where our sustenance is not aligned with the essence of what we are. Consequently we are losing touch with our essence and becoming a product of that which sustains an *image* of existence- existence without human essence. (Ever heard the phrase "This is inhuman?") Furthermore, we have developed machine entities called computers that are even better products of our *image of existence;* i.e. computers are an even "better caterpillar" relative to the reality we are evolving. The result is no real need or "place" for humanity because the very essence of humanity is not being nurtured.

Sustenance and essence, if aligned, are a powerful force toward survival. For example, the very essence of a tiger is agility, claws and teeth. These are also the very things that sustain it. The agility, claws and teeth are used for catching and eating the food that sustains it. Sustenance is aligned with essence. This alignment prevails in all animals and plants. In humanity it is becoming more and more separated. If sustenance and essence become fully separated in a creature, that creature will simply fade from existence. Separation of sustenance and essence makes survival a struggle. Alignment of sustenance and essence makes survival *a song sung while living.*

We must survive long enough to learn adaptation.
We must adapt in order to evolve.
We must evolve in order to return to God.

The Folly
This misalignment of sustenance and essence has kept us from really finding and knowing ourselves. Not knowing ourselves has left us without connection or direction and the result is the folly of modern humanity.

There has long been talk of the folly of modern humanity in "re-inventing the wheel." What if we take that thought a few steps further? If it is folly to re-invent the wheel, isn't it folly to re-invent the earth or re-invent nature? I would venture to say that everything we *need* for quite luxurious survival already appears in nature. I would further venture to say that much of this is being destroyed in the process of re-inventing it. Wouldn't it seem crazy to destroy the wheel and all memory of it in the process of re-inventing one not quite as good as the original?

Our human ingenuity has become a ravaging beast in search of itself. *It is time for more intuitive encounters with the earth, the elements, and the universe.* This will equalize human ingenuity as a force on this planet. Human ingenuity, if allowed to continue on its present course, will soon result in a computer that gets up and tells its programmer to get off at the next stop. After all, computers don't need clean air or fresh water. Not only will we not be needed in the new world we are creating, we won't be able to survive there anyway.

We find ourselves struggling with the problems this folly has created while not seeing the folly itself. It is quite possible there will continue to be semi-workable, temporary solutions to these problems. However, it is not really the effects of the folly that must be overcome, it is human life itself.

Being a victim of the problems of the human condition results in a grounding effect. It is necessary to disconnect from the strong grounding effects of the swarm of humanity. These grounding effects tunnel our vision and keep our energies entirely "swarm" oriented. The disconnecting must take place gradually because our minds and bodies, for generations, have been manipulated by swarm attitudes. These swarm attitudes make it next to impossible to live any other way except the way the swarm lives. Strong individual energies effect the swarm attitudes. However, the swarm continues to evolve ruthlessly as its own massive entity. Thus to effectively leave it- escape from it and become familiar with other dimensions relative to earth and sky- we must phase out of the human swarm in stages.

To facilitate this "phasing out" I suggest we observe ourselves from a greater distance. This distance must be in space and time and far from the swarm of humanity that now surrounds us. Here we will see our "place" in an ever-evolving universe. Here we will learn about expanded evolution.

PASS SLOWLY THROUGH THE
NETWORK OF LOOSELY WOVEN
    REALITIES.

DO NOT ALLOW YOURSELF TO
SNAG ON ANY SINGLE
    THREAD.

THE SPACES BETWEEN THESE
THREADS ARE THE SPACES THAT
WILL LET YOU FLOAT UNATTACHED
THROUGH ANY "REAL WORLD"
    SNAGS.

YOUR INHERENT MAGIC - YOUR
ENERGY BAND - WILL THEN STEER
YOU TO DIMENSIONS BEYOND YOUR
    WILDEST DREAM.

WHERE NO THREADS OF REALITY
    EXIST
WHERE MULTI-DIRECTIONAL FORCES
    PLAY
WHERE TIME IS NOT
WHERE MATTER IS NOT.

JUST A GLIMPSE OF THIS WILL
REDUCE THE GRIP OF THE REAL
WORLD SWARM AND ALLOW YOUR
ENERGY TO FLOOD, UNRESTRAINED,
THROUGH THE REAL WORLD AND
    BEYOND.

Once there was earth
    all plush and green
    all hot and steaming
    all wet and dreaming
    animals coasting
    music living
    life so giving

Once there was us
    all brave and learning
    passions burning
    lusts all churning
    desires all showing
    love exposing
    hatred glowing
    numbers growing

We defined beauty
    awesome and pure
    then pursued it until
    it existed no more

Earth defined us
    evolving and reaching
    to define our new beauty
    while our old beauty's weeping.

I SAW THE BRIGHT STARS SHINING
PHANTOMS IN THE SKY
I SAW THE WHITE STAR OF TOMORROW
I SAW A BLACK STAR DIE

I AM NOW A MAN OF MIDNIGHT
ONE FIRE LIGHTS MY WAY
TO NOTHING, EVERYTHING IS SOMETHING
THE SAME IS TRUE TODAY

I SAW A SIMPLE SILENT CREATURE
GRAZING ON THE PLAIN
IT GREW INTO A COMPLEX BEAST
AND THEN CAME BACK AGAIN

TRAVELING WEST INTO THE HALF MOON
TOOK ME MUCH TOO FAR TOO FAST
I WAS DEEP INTO THE FUTURE
I WAS DEEP INTO THE PAST

I WATCHED TEN THOUSAND YEARS GO BY
AND PLOTTED WHAT I COULD
IF I TOLD YOU OF THE PATTERNS THEREI
YOU WOULD NOT HAVE UNDERSTOOD

YOUR PAST HAS FORMED YOUR FUTURE
YOU HAVE ORGANIZED YOUR YEARS
YOUR SWORDS HAVE KILLED YOUR DRAGONS
YOU HAVE ORGANIZED YOUR FEARS

YOU'LL CHOKE YOURSELF WITH YOUR OWN HANDS
AND FAINT BEFORE YOU DIE
THEN SUFFER FROM THE PAIN YOU CAUSED
AND SIT AND WONDER WHY

IT'S HARD FOR ME TO STAND BESIDE YOU
KNOWING WHAT YOU'LL DO
AND KNOWING HOW FUCKED-UP YOU'LL BE
BEFORE YOUR HANDS ARE THROUGH

FORGIVE ME IF I CHOOSE TO LEAVE
FORGIVE ME IF I TRY
FOR I SAW A BRIGHT STAR SHINING
AND I'M HEADING FOR THE SKY.

**Knowledge is a ghost
that haunts the learned.**

CHAPTER TWO
A LINK WITH LIGHT

Earthbound spirits
cruise at low altitudes.

There's a fire in my eyes
I can't see you for the flame

And if your heart caresses me
It may be all in vain

And if your arrows strike me
They may not cause me pain

I'm going through the motions
But I've slipped out of the game.

Unarguable Phenomenon

Slipping out of the game (the dogmas of the swarm of humanity) is necessary in order to move out of a limiting reality and on to a more expanded view of ourselves and how we relate to the universe. If we look away from dogmas and toward *unarguable phenomenon*, we will find guidance. These unarguable phenomenon can show us more about ourselves, as we too, are a phenomenon.

Dogmas like capitalism, socialism, Catholicism, Protestantism, etc. and even humanism, seem to run our lives. Unarguable phenomenon like the sun "rising" in the east and "setting" in the west, are the *reason we are alive.* Maybe we should give a little more consideration to these than to our dogmas. No one argues with, votes about, or forbids the rising or the setting of the sun. All races, sexes, animals and plants simply accept all aspects of it without argument- it is a truth. The sun shines the same for all life forms without judgment, prejudice or corruption; all of which exist within our dogmas. If we relate much more intensely to the various unarguable phenomenon in the universe, we will break out of our human situation and into a more "road-worthy" form for exploring the universe.

Our dogmas tell us what we are and we believe them. These dogmas crowd out the imagination in our dreams, the inspiration from the cosmos, and the intuition from our genes. What if an eagle was somehow more influenced by an earthbound dogma than by its own intuitive forces and, consequently, did not have mental "space" for awareness of its wings and what they were for. The dogma would actually keep it from experiencing flight, which is really what a bird of any kind is all about. I believe that our human dogmas fill our mind space and crowd out our imaginative, inspirational, and intuitive forces, thus, keeping us from experiencing "flight" in the universe, which is what we are all about.

To experience this flight, i.e. to journey beyond our present reality, we must "slip out of the game" and lean toward the truths of unarguable phenomenon. Our relationship, our link, to these unarguable phenomenon can then be thoroughly explored, thus, leading to a synthesis of these unarguable phenomenon and ourselves.

Light is an unarguable phenomenon. An exploration of light can lead deep into quantum physics. Some physicists believe that all matter is "trying to return to light" as it has been put in Fred Allen Wolf's book, *Star Wave.* They say that matter is basically trapped or condensed light. One would think if we could return to light, we could "travel" all around the universe. However, "travel" seems to be simply our word; and futhermore, the speed of light is not that "fast" relative to the unfanthomable distances of the universe.

Further exploration of energy and matter, both relatives of light, takes us to the electron. Electrons orbit or swarm around protons and nutrons (the nucleus) thus forming atoms. However, electrons can be unattached to any nucleus, thus existing as "free-bodies" so to speak. A very awesome unarguable phenomenon involving the electron has been unveiled but not quite understood by physicists in the last few decades. It is an *instantaneous awareness* between electrons. This is not a "communication" at the speed of light, but simply an awareness that is instantaneous. This phenomenon has been called "non-local awareness" and the seventh chapter of this book has been devoted to it. Suffice it to say now, that the very existence of the phenomenon of non-local awareness itself, emphasizes the potential of pursuing our link with light.

Stars

Light is related to both matter and energy and thus encompasses everything. Therefore, our search for understanding and interaction with this unarguable phenomenon, light, could guide us in a search for ourselves - our potential.

A major source of visible light in the universe is the stars - stars both like and unlike our own sun. Stable main sequence stars are very basically masses of gas compressed enough by their own gravity to create intense heat. This heat reaches such extremes that nuclear fusion takes place releasing energy that further heats the gas to create an expanding outward pressure that balances the inward pull of the gravity. Our sun is such a star - in perfect balance of expansion and contraction. Stars that do not achieve and maintain this balance contract into black holes or burn themselves out. Black holes are stars whose gravity became so strong that nothing, not even light, could escape them. Consequently, they are invisible points in our universe. The gravity of our human situation, our introverted evolution, is becoming so strong that we are headed toward a black hole situation.

Astrophysics can guide us in exploring psycophysics. The same patterns apply. Human energy, when realizing its full potential, can achieve a natural balance similar to that of the stars. With this balance we can blaze like a stable sun emitting life-giving energy for all that surrounds us. We have to expand and extend ourselves enough to create a type of "human fusion." This fusion will release an expansive energy to counter-balance our own gravity both as individuals and as a society or civilization. The swarm of humanity however is neither expanding nor "fusing" at this point and consequently our "light" is not escaping. We are becoming victims of our own gravity. We are becoming black holes, invisible to the universe. This may be why we have not had much contact at the scientific level with the consciousness of the universe. Our gadgets are probing "out there" but our minds remain "in here"; caged in an introverted reality, cut off from the mind of the universe (of which it is a part) by our dogmas. The fire from within, our energy band, if we will make space for it in our beings, will "heat" us to the point of "fusion," thus creating an expansive energy to equalize our own gravity/ego/selfness/swarm. Like our sun, we can be a stable phenomenon.

The natural balance of a stable phenomenon can be a model for what has been called karma in the human condition. Expansion resulting from "human fusion" can equalize the gravity of the human condition. "Human fusion" (similar to nuclear fusion) means interaction with others in such a way that expansion occurs. For example: when two people lift a log they have expanded the "fused" strength beyond that of either individual. In our reality this fusion only happens on occasion. We must learn to live in a state of fusion, if we are to expand beyond the human condition. Fusion spawns expansion.

"Good karma" is the balance with inherent gravity that expansion achieves. By not expanding, we are allowing the gravity of the human condition to take us into introverted evolution and eventually into a "black hole." This resulting imbalance is what we call "bad karma." It is our responsibility to find our energy, our energy band, to claim it and to fuse and expand with it. We thereby *create* our karma, our balance. Otherwise the imbalance - the gravity - "bad karma" manipulates and "creates" *us.* *Karma is, in effect, the forces of nature reacting to the "choices" we make regarding balance.* We have the potential (choice) to become a "balanced star." We are a potential source of energy. However, *karma/nature will take us if we don't take ourselves.*

This balance of expansion and contraction is found in our breathing as well as at both extremes of the universe. Atoms actually expand in little "quantum leaps" where the electron changes its relationship to the nucleus and leaps or pops out to another probable location. This is called an "excited state" and is the way an atom interacts with other atoms to form molecules. This involves the sharing of electrons as atoms "hold hands" so to speak to form something more than an atom. *Thus, it is the expansion of the atom that allows it to be more than an atom.* So it is with the human. Our expansion allows us to be more than human.

The universe itself is believed to be expanding. Astrophysics has shown us that all stars and galaxies are moving away from each other. Many astrophysicists believe the universe has been expanding since the "big bang" (a theory on how the universe was born) and that it will expand to a certain point, then contract again to a giant black hole, only to explode again in another "big bang." Thus, the pulsation or expansion and contraction is found at both extremes of our physical awareness.

This expansion and contraction is an unarguable phenomenon. It is a dance that the universe is doing. We can synthesize ourselves with this dance. This means movement and maneuverability. This means dropping our fixed dogmas - dropping ourselves.

As I plunge into selflessness
I can hear the demons scream

For it is on bridges of self interest
That they go from hell into my dreams.

"As above - so below." We can see that stars are doing the same dance as the atom and the universe itself. This being the dance of expansion and contraction - a pulsation. Stars represent what is happening at both extremes of the universe. They are our guides. They are showing us what we are beyond the human form, which itself is simply a dogma. Stars are our angels - lights that can guide us toward light itself and beyond. They exist without dogma. They are unarguable phenomenon to lean toward and relate to throughout our journey. They are raw energy - light. That "flicker" or "energy" inside us is the "star angel" wanting to be born.

Stars are expressions of consciousness throughout the universe.

Stars manifest and support many forms of consciousness, one of which we call "life" and have attached a dogma called humanity to it. Our search for "life" in other solar systems and galaxies is not as pertinent as a search for consciousness within ourselves. We have to attain consciousness ourselves before we can find it, or even recognize it, in the universe. We are presently spending considerable energy searching for other "human-oid" creatures in the universe. Maybe there are some, but that could be like being a snowflake and searching for another identically like yourself. The *chemistry* of snowflakes is where the commonalty is, not the geometric pattern of the snowflake. Likewise, *the alchemy of consciousness is where the commonality is between us and the universe*, not the physical form we have taken here. Consciousness does not necessarily mean two-legged creatures.

To take these bodies - these dogmas - to the heavens is absurd. You wouldn't take your house with you on a trip around the world, so why must we take the human form on a trip around the universe? We are not trapped in our house. Or are we? We are not trapped in our bodies. Or are we? We have become so attached to both houses and bodies that we have ceased to hear the message in the stars.

Stars reach out to communicate with us with light but we have forgotten our "native tongue." We are basically light encapsulated in a dogma that we have spun around ourselves. Possibly, this dogma has been an incubator somewhat like a cocoon. We can break out of the cocoon any time now and be "butterflies" or we can rot in the cocoon. Stars are bidding us to leave the cocoon. They are communicating to each other and to us constantly via light. They are also "non-locally aware" of the universe as a whole. We, for the most part, are not even aware of the phenomenon of "non-local awareness." This leaves us "in" the human situation.

I have, throughout this book, presented many examples of automatic writing (often in the form of poetry). These writings and my research into quantum and astro physics in order to "justify" what was being said, has left me with the feeling that stars are our heavenly fathers. Their "voices" can be heard inside us if only we would make space for them by dumping our dogmas.

Stars are consciousness. They are angels. We are the descendants of stars.

Path of the Star Angel

Openness
> recognition of unarguable phenomenon
> exploration of all patterns of the cosmos
> awareness in all aspects of consciousness

Communication
> ability to find and go to commonalty
> levels of all things

Peace
> all living things self-destruct except
> those who can and will grasp their energy band
> and reflect it and be it.
> these will live in peace and harmony
> in the motion of the universe.

Unity
> peace and harmony will fuse all living things into unity,
> living things will fuse with non-living things

Expansion occurs.

Energy is produced.

Energy and matter dance.

Star Angels are born.

Prayer to My Fathers

Eyes that see the road
When there's really no road there
Hands that shape a future
When there's future everywhere
Heart that shields all sorrow
Yet still feels every pain.

Oh my father and my fathers
I feel you once again

Threads all weaving through me
Coming from your souls
Make me hear tomorrow's bell
Long before it tolls
Flawless though I'm not
As I stumble and complain.

Oh my father and my fathers
I feel you once again.

Message From Father Sun

Give times threat of death
    a chance to crest many times
    before you leave

Take past terms of life as memories only
    for they have no link with tomorrow

Want just for the crown of stars in the sky
Kill only the thought of sorrow

Live all days and nights
Think everything twice
Fly all the air motions before you

You're touching the sun
Your fire has begun
You'll have planets all swirling around you.

SOMEWHERE NEAR THE EDGE
I SAW MY REFLECTION

SOMEWHERE NEAR THE EDGE
IT WAS SMILING BACK AT ME

SOMEWHERE NEAR THE EDGE
I SAW THE DECEPTION

OF THE PAST AND THE FUTURE
AND THE MEMORY. . .

CRIPPLED ON THE EARTH
I FLEW MUCH HIGHER

BLINDED BY DECEPTION
I BEGAN TO SEE

LEFT OUT IN THE COLD
I BECAME A FIRE

THE DAWNING OF AWARENESS
BURNING NOW INSIDE OF ME.

Vision

I met in a vision with some entities that came to earth from afar. There were lots of beings milling around and casually communicating. It reminded me of a cocktail party situation. No actual words were spoken, as communication was beyond the actual scope of words. All the beings were humanoid types. They looked strange with unusual features, but the upright body concept was common to all. I remember two or three specific creatures and what they communicated about travel in the universe.

They made an analogy around common denominators or commonalty. Water is a common denominator among all human bodies; they are all roughly 88% water. The earth is a water planet. Water is thus, also a common denominator between all human bodies and the earth. It is reasonably easy to conceive of breaking the human body down through chemical processes to just a small pile of organic matter and a few gallons of water. Water travels all over the planet. It runs, rises, falls, evaporates, freezes and condenses. *The mobility of the human body around the earth is much more restricted than the mobility of water.*

Light, they explained, is a common denominator between human "life" and the universe. The energy we call "life" is a form of light. This can be confirmed through modern physics as we know it. The human body is made up of water and organic matter. Both of which can be reduced to basic elements and finally to atoms. Most of the very atoms that make up the human body are common all over the universe. Certain natural forces within these atoms, explored through quantum physics, are actually a common denominator of all atoms. These forces within the atom that have to do with holding it together and joining it with other atoms are a form of raw energy, of which light is simply a visible manifestation. This raw energy, or light as we know it, is common all over the universe just as water is common all over our planet earth. Water travels and "is" all over the earth. Light travels and "is" all over the universe. Just as we can be physically reduced to water, we can also be physically reduced to light. This "light" never really dies. It changes back and forth from matter to energy, but is always conserved. Both atomic physics and modern religion seem to agree on this. Thus, like the situation with water, *the mobility of the human body around the universe is much more restricted than the mobility of light.*

The "group" I met with traveled through the universe as a form of light. One, two, or many individual entities were "mixed" together, just as the water making up several different humans could be mixed together. They traveled through the universe as "one light." They have acquired the actualization of the concept of unity we only talk about here. **Unity cannot be totally achieved in the form- only through the commonality.**

Upon entering the plane of existence of an energy harbor, such as Earth, spheres of white light were surrounded by what were called "energy transformation screens." The accompanying diagram illustrates one of the many transformation screens I saw in my encounter. Through these screens, "life light" (organized consciousness) can take form appropriate to the specific chemistry of the particular energy harbor (planet or other heavenly body) it has entered. We are light. We meet mass in a "plane of existence" relative to our energy harbor - the earth. Thus we are born.

WE CAN TRAVEL AS A FORM OF LIGHT TO OTHER ENERGY HARBORS THROUGHOUT THE COSMOS. WHEN WE REACH A PLANE OF EXISTANCE RELATIVE TO A PARTICULAR ENERGY HARBOR, WE MATERIALIZE (VIA THE ENERGY TRANSFORMATION SCREENS OF THE PLANE OF EXISTANCE OF THAT HARBOR) IN A SUITABLE"BODY" FOR THAT PARTICULAR ENERGY HARBOR. THIS SOUNDS A BIT LIKE BIRTH AND DEATH AS WE KNOW IT. IT OCCURED TO ME THE "GROUP" I ENCOUNTERED COULD HAVE BEEN WHAT WE CALL UNBORN SOULS.

"Seeing" happens without eyes

"Flying" happens without wings

"Being" happens without form

 Energy is you.

You've got to learn
    to live by the instant

Because that is the way
    paradise comes.

The Eternal Present

Experiments in physics have proven that as we move toward the speed of light time slows down and *at the* speed of light (300,000 km/sec) time would stop.

The vibration rate of the caesuim atom is now our most accurate time scale. Caesium atomic clocks have been used to verify the speeding up and slowing down of time relative to velocity. This has also been verified by mathematical equations developed by Einstein and other noted physicists.

The graph opposite illustrates how time "slows down" as velocity increases. The bottom horizontal scale of the graph goes from zero velocity to 300,000 km/sec, the speed of light. This illustrates all possible speeds conceivable in our "present" reality since speed beyond the speed of light is deemed impossible for matter. Einstein's $E=MC^2$ theory currently seems to prove this. Zero velocity(stopped) is obviously the slowest we can go, as a negative velocity (going backwards) still simply represents movement at a velocity. Therefore, zero km/sec to 300,000 km/sec covers all possible velocities.

The vertical scale on the graph is the speed of time. It goes from zero (time stopped) to our normal speed of time - that is the speed of time (i.e. the vibration rate of the caesium atom) at zero velocity on earth. However, the surface of the earth is spinning at approximately .46 km/sec.. The earth is also revolving around the sun at approximately 29.9 km/sec.. The sun is revolving around the center of the Milky Way at a approximately 250 km/sec. If these speeds were all moving in the same direction simultaneously (which is possible), their total velocity would be 280 km/sec. This is not to mention that our galaxy itself is moving according to the proven theory of the expanding universe. Consequently, a caesium atom clock on the earth can hardly be deemed to have zero velocity. 280 km/sec. is shown on the horizontal velocity scale of the graph. Even though it is negligible (relative to the speed of light), it illustrates that "true time" (time unaffected by velocity) is impossible because we can't find a non-moving place to put a caesium atomic clock.

The graphed curve indicates a drop in the speed of time as velocity increases. It is deduced that the curve never touches either the vertical or the horizontal scales because both zero velocity and the speed of light are impossible relative to earth and matter.

Time stands still at the speed of light, therefore, an *eternal present* is the result of the speed of light. Past and future are simply different aspects of the eternal present, isolated and experienced from a "position" that is out of sync with the speed of light. From a position beyond the speed of light, we would see various pasts. From a position slower than the speed of light, we would see various futures. Since we are moving (on earth) at a approximately 200-280 km/sec (slower than light) we are actually existing in a future aspect of the eternal present. This is why we can't seem to get to the eternal present, i.e. "everlasting life" as the Bible puts it. As long as we are confined to the material state, we are stuck in the isolated aspect of the eternal present that we call the future.

The nature of the atom shows us that matter can be transformed into energy. Energy can move at the speed of light - energy is light. Energy lives in the eternal present. *Time, future and past, only exists as a result of our material form being "out of sync" with light.* As we bring our material form into sync with light (i.e. allow our energy band to prevail), we move toward the eternal present where we have access to all futures and all pasts. We must come to know the energy aspect of ourselves so we can move as light.

MOVING AS LIGHT IS EXEMPLIFIED BY THE EXPERIMENT OF GRAVITY: A MAN JUMPS OFF A CLIFF WITH A ROCK IN HIS HAND. WHILE HE IS FALLING, HE DROPS THE ROCK. HE FINDS THAT THE ROCK DOES NOT FALL OR MOVE RELATIVE TO HIM- SELF. THEY ARE BOTH "IN FALL" TOGETHER. NO UP - NO DOWN - NO SEPARATION.

IF WE WOULD ALLOW THE ENERGY ASPECT OF OURSELVES TO PREVAIL, WE WOULD FIND OURSELVES *IN LIGHT* (AS ENLIGHTENED). HERE WE WOULD FIND THE PRESENT LIKE THE ROCK - IT WOULD STAY WITH US. NO SEPARATION. IN OUR CURRENT SIT- UATION ON EARTH, BOTH ROCKS AND THE PRESENT SEEM TO SLIP AWAY FROM US. IN LIGHT, THE PRESENT WOULD BE ETERNAL.

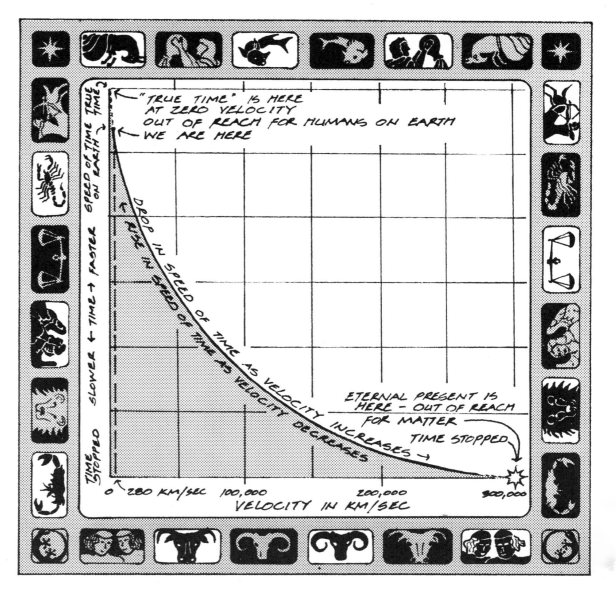

Experiments in physics have also concluded that time slows down in stronger gravitational fields. Therefore, "true time" would occur in a situation totally unaffected by any gravity, and time would stop (creating the eternal present) where gravity is very intense.

This phenomenon has also been proven with the caesium atomic clock. Two caesium atomic clocks were used. One was placed outside the earth's gravitational field in an orbiting satellite, while the other was placed on the surface of the earth where gravitation is significantly stronger. When the satellite returned, the two clocks were compared and the orbiting clock having experienced the lesser gravity was found to be ahead of the earth clock.

This experiment has also been verified mathematically in equations developed by Einstein.

The graph opposite illustrates how time slows down as gravity increases. It is basically the same graph as the previous one. It illustrates the same phenomenon, time stopping in an eternal present with us trapped in a future. However, here it is a function of gravity rather than velocity. Thus we have, from two different vantage points (gravity and velocity) arrived at the same conclusion.

The basic difference between this graph and the previous one is that the horizontal scale (which indicated velocity of matter) has been replaced by a hypothetical scale indicating the *density* of matter, of which strength of gravitational field is a function. Thus, we have a horizontal scale illustrating gravity getting stronger and a vertical scale illustrating time speeding up (the vertical scale being the same as before.)

The horizontal scale goes from zero gravity, which we do not have on earth, to the most intense gravity that can be comprehended or imagined. This is the gravity of a black hole, which is so strong that light itself cannot escape it. Relative to this, our gravitational field on earth would appear close to zero, just as our velocity appeared close to zero relative to the speed of light on the previous graph. The curve on this graph can be deduced to be similar. Time drops in speed until it finally stops at the density and intense gravitation of a black hole. Light is trapped here and time is stopped here. We, in the human form, cannot exist in a black hole, so for us the situation is impossible. With time stopped here, we again find an eternal present, unavailable to us in the human form. If we accept the fact that "time stopped" does indicate an eternal present, then moving time again represents isolated aspects of that eternal present, thus placing us in a situation called future on one side of the eternal present and allowing a situation called past on the other side of the eternal present. (This is strictly confining our discussion to the two dimensions of the graph). Just as in the discussion on the previous page it is quite impossible for us, in the human condition, to experience absolute zero velocity due to the movement within and of our solar system. It is also quite impossible for us to experience, in the human condition, absolute zero gravity for similar reasons. Even when we are outside of the earth's gravity, we are still under the influence of the sun's gravity as the earth itself is. Therefore, gravity would still be influencing time to some extent anywhere in our solar system. Then our solar system is under the influence of the gravity of the Milky Way Galaxy. Thus is appears that zero gravity, like zero velocity, is a nonexistent situation in our pulsating universe. Therefore the curve on the graph does not touch the vertical scale. This leaves "true time", (time not influenced by either gravity or velocity) unattainable. This indicates that time itself, i.e. anything outside of the eternal present, is an illusion. Since time speeds up as both gravity and velocity approach zero, true time would be infinitely fast, because there is no end to how far we can project into the illusion of the future.

AGAIN, THE PRESENT (TIME STOP-PED) SEEMS TO BE IN A PLACE THAT WE CAN'T REACH IN OUR CURRENT MATERIAL STATE. THE FUTURE (TIME SPEEDING UP) IS WHERE WE ARE. BLACK HOLES AND THE SPEED OF LIGHT KEEP THE PRESENT EVER ILLUSIVE - A RAINBOW WE CAN'T CATCH UP TO IN THE MATERIAL FORM.

WE HAVE, IN TERMS OF MODERN PHYSICS, FOUND AN ETERNAL PRE-SENT - A PLACE OF "EVERLASTING LIFE" SPOKEN ABOUT IN THE BIBLE. APPROACHING THIS PLACE UN-CONSCIOUSLY IN THE HUMAN FORM COULD BE HELL. HOWEVER, CONSCIOUSLY APPROACHING IT VIA THE ENERGY ASPECT OF OUR-SELVES COULD BE WHAT HAS BEEN CALLED HEAVEN.

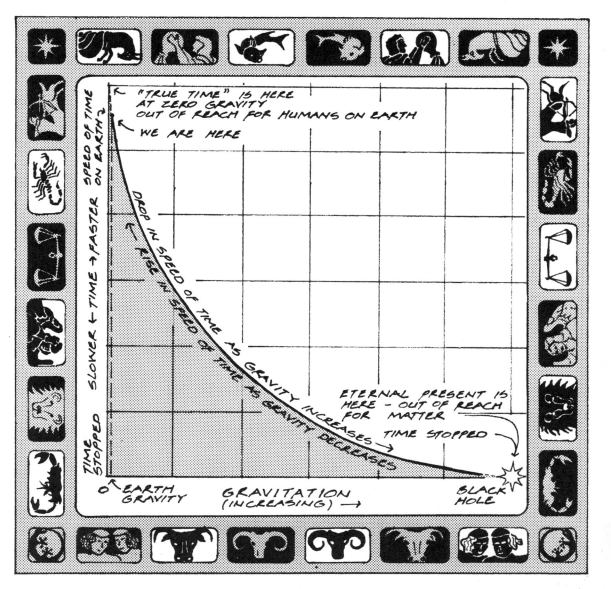

If the eternal present is paradise. . .
And if this paradise contains *all*
    pasts, presents, and futures. . .

Everything we experience is a "piece of Paradise."

It is simply our isolation of this "piece of Paradise"
    that creates the illusion of something
    other than Paradise.

Time has come to say that you're not lonely
Time has come to say you're not the only
Time has come to help you
        plant the seed that you can't find
Time will take your hand
Time will take your mind

Time has been your father
        the force that pulled you through
Time has been your mother
        caressing, holding you
Time has been your lover
        though soon to set you free
Time will be yourself
If you want it to be

Time has held your karma in reflecting glass
        for you
Time will give it back when you least
        expect it to
Time saw the beginning and time will see
        the end
Time will recognize you
When you come back again.

Incredible Journey - Easter 1975

I have a coffer up on top of my pyramid in the canyon. Sometimes I would climb up to it and strap myself in and gaze at the full moon all night long from the apex of the pyramid. One Easter night this "vehicle" took me on an incredible journey.

With no more than a flicker, like a tape mistracking, I was suddenly gone. I didn't realize I was gone until I returned three days later. The "me" that was left behind these three days wandered around in a stupor and was capable of very little. It was as if everything positive about me left for three days.

I recall:
A glow that wasn't light
An intense hum that wasn't noise
They surrounded me just for a moment as elements began pouring out of my body like a swarm of bees leaving a hive all at once together, unable to resist the invitation of pollens in the air from a nearby apple tree in blossom.

I am no longer "I". I am no longer "me". My elements diffused among the positive of the positives of this planet.

There were other balls of life-like earth from which these amoebic-like swarms of elements came. All swarms had a glow that was not light and a hum that was not sound. Some were different colors. Some were white and some were black, a black glow. I have no idea which one "I" was in. I didn't know who. I didn't know what. I didn't care.

The swarms all funnelled into a whirlpool-like void in the side of the sky, the sky not relative to the earth. There was a feeling here - a strong, deep, nearly off-balanced, stimulating, close to unbearable feeling. But there was no **body** to be registering this feeling. This feeling **was**. It filled the void. It seemed a place as illusive and beautiful as a rainbow, yet it was truly a tangible feeling. To be the swarm diffusing and collecting with other swarms. To be in the void. To be this feeling.

Using words or graphics to describe it is like trying to part your hair with a pipe wrench - you simply make a gesture.

The void seemed to be a screening and/or charging or energizing place. Most elements of the feeling seemed to get charged and sparked out of the void directly back to the ball of life from which they came as a swarm. They seemed to be individually attracted, as if by a magnet, back to the ball of life from which they came. This is the process through which "I" would return, an element at a time. Each element that returned had many times the **presence** it had upon leaving. All the elements that left did not return. However, if only half of them did, "I" would still be coming back as more than I was when "I" left.

Some elements stayed. They stayed in the void. Not many of mine I suspect, but a few did.

It seemed that occasionally, some constantly remaining elements of the feeling left through the void to what must be the other side of the sky.

There seemed to be a misty slag or foam around the void. It seemed to be the fine contaminated traces of other energies that were bathed off, so to speak, in the void.

THE VOID SEEMS TO BE A FINAL PURIFICATION PLACE BEFORE GOING TO THE OTHER SIDE OF THE SKY.

THIS JOURNEY INVOLVED ONLY THE ENERGY ASPECT OF MYSELF. I BELIEVE I WAS WITHIN "SIGHT" OF THE ETERNAL PRESENT. I WITNESSED RAW ENERGY APPROACHING AND SOMETIMES ENTERING THE ETERNAL PRE-PRESENT. I WITNESSED THE COMING AND GOING OF ENERGY FROM EARTH AND OTHER ENERGY HARBORS. I WAS IN THE MELTING POT OF BIRTH, DEATH AND ETERNAL LIFE.

Can you touch the glow of morning
    as it drifts into a day
Can you be the mighty mountain
    when you need to be that way
Can you see the God of Thunder
    as he rolls across the sky
Can you see he's dropping flower peddles
    down on you and I
Can you feel the reeling energy
    from every living thing
Can you see it makes us happy
Can you see it makes us sing

Can you see into the rainbow
Can you see into the wind
Can you see into the starlight
Can you see into your friend
Can you yield into the moonlight
Can it penetrate your eyes
Can you see it makes us peaceful
Can you see it makes us high

Can you peel away your dogma
Can you peel away your fear
Can you see your journey's ending
Can you see it started here
Can you pass into the spirit
Can you send it with your eye
Can you see it makes us rise up
Can you see it makes us fly

Come fly with me.

CHAPTER THREE
WHERE MIND
AND MATTER MEET

Illusive and flashing the magic appears
It commands full attention
                    it won't allow fear

Earth is a mirror of magic and matter
Both sides look the same
                    but one side will shatter

Drift with the moonlight
Fly with the sun
When truth shines around you
                    magic will come

If you form it or hold it or mentally mold it
It fades like a dream
                    before you have told it

Somewhere between your eyes
                    and the things that they see
The essence of magic is waiting to be

Drift with the moonlight
Fly with the sun
When truth shines around you
                    magic will come.

Fritjof Capra, in his book, **The Tao of Physics,** says we are approaching "A field of research where patterns of matter and patterns of mind are increasingly being recognized as reflections of one another."

The topic of mind and matter has been covered in many books for many years by physicists and philosophers and mystics. It is not the aim of this chapter to simply re-present the already existing thought that mind and matter could or possibly do meet. It is, however, necessary to briefly discuss this thought in an effort to *establish a frame of reference near the extremities of existing dogma* from which we can get the best possible "view" of the material presented in the following chapters.

No one has fully explained or discovered exactly how mind and matter meet simply because we still do not know exactly what mind or matter is. The fact remains that the deeper we penetrate the subatomic world, the more matter appears related to mind, and mind appears to be a non-personal phenomenon that we all have *limited* access to. It is our limited access to mind that keeps us from the "place" *where mind and matter* meet, or it could be said that our limits keep us from the "place" where mind and matter *are the same*. This book is, in part, about alleviating these limits. It is therefore necessary to try and project hypothetically, where and/or what this "place" might be in preparation for discussing how to alleviate the limits that keep us from it.

The Arena of Mutual Participation
All the macroworld sciences, taken to their lowest common denominator, end up in the microworld. This microworld begins with the atom. The atom is made up of a nucleus with electrons swarming around it. This nucleus is made up of tiny bits of matter called haydrons. There seems to be an infinite number of different types of haydrons, of which the proton and neutron are the most common. The haydrons are divided into two categories relative to their units of spin; the meson (its spin is measured in whole integers) and the bayron (its spin is measured in half integers). Recently the haydrons have been found to be made up of quarks, of which there are five, maybe six or more different types. It is quite possible the quarks are made up of something even smaller but current technology cannot deal with anything smaller than a quark at this point.

Matter can be changed into energy and visa-versa. This microworld containing tiny bits of matter/energy from the atomic nucleus down to the quark and beyond also possibly consist of four different kinds of natural forces that could, in the future, all be found to be different aspects of the same force. The forces are currently called electromagnetic, strong nuclear, weak nuclear, and gravitation.

It is here in the subatomic world that the laws of classical and determinist physics all begin to cease to apply. Here we are entering what is called *quantum reality*. Very simply, the particles in the microworld are so small that they no longer behave like particles. This situation is something like the difference between a rock falling and a piece of goose down falling. The rock falls straight down while the piece of goose down drifts and meanders as it falls. It is so light that it is affected by the air it is falling through and consequently takes on some of the characteristics of the air, i.e. currents etc. Matter, in its subatomic realm, seems to be like the goose down; it takes on some of the characteristics of the currents around it. *These currents are the currents of mind.*

This gives us a very simplified graphic analogy of the "place" we are talking about. Let it be called an arena - **an arena of mutual participation.** This is an arena where both mind and matter participate in what ends up being called a reality.

Thus far men have seen themselves as "in the stands" of this arena "watching" what has been created. They have not realized the degree to which they are unknowingly participating. This is due to our limited access to mind. We have to accept the fact that we ourselves, and our macroworld, are a result of this mutual participation. Indeed, we *are* both mind and matter. However, we tend to dwell in either the mind or the material, not realizing or accepting their oneness. It is we who have created the illusion of isolation between mind and matter. This is like being a two-legged creature hopping along on one leg at a time- first one leg then the other. In fact, two-legged creatures can use *both* legs simultaneously in a unified motion, thus gaining much greater mobility. Likewise, if we dwell in mind and matter in a "unified motion" (this is the arena of mutual participation) we can gain much more mobility in the universe and the multi-universe.[1]

The arena of mutual participation is available to us. It is where mind and matter are the same. It is from here we must operate in order to reach our potential.

---

[1] There are whispers these days, from more than one source, of a multiverse, i.e. our universe is not the only one.

In the subatomic world we have found that by releasing a little control over energy, we gain a little control over matter, and by releasing a little control over matter we gain a little control over energy. This is the result of various experiments and observations involving the conversion of matter to energy and energy to matter. Operating from the arena of mutual participation involves a similar "dance." By releasing our "grip" on mind we allow matter, and by releasing our "grip" on matter we allow mind. This is like walking - first one foot and then the other. Thus we can walk through the universe.

Conscious Participation

In the quantum reality, particals of matter sometimes behave like waves of energy and they don't follow any rigid set of rules about what they will do and when they will do it. This randomness has perplexed modern day physicists. However, it is this randomness that has facilitated nature's reaching out to the *isolated aspect of mind possessed by humankind*. We experience our thoughts through mind. These thoughts have a randomness similar to the randomness found in the subatomic world. Matter takes on the characteristics of these thoughts, as goose down takes on the characteristics of air, and visa-versa. It is in this exchange that "a common language" is spoken via minute electrical charges. Mind and matter, both aspects of humanity, interact charge for charge in the arena of mutual participation. We must coax our egos to let us leave the "sidelines" and consciously get into the game. Conscious *participation* in nature would seem to have many more possibilities than our current game of unconscious *manipulation* of nature. Unconscious manipulation suggests separation of human and nature while conscious participation suggests both are one. If we accept that we *are* nature, we can more adeptly participate. This concious participation is how we effect our evolution and increase our access to mind.

To facilitate our participation in the phenomenon of mind and matter let us construct a simple model. Everyone has seen how the tiny iron shavings on a piece of paper can be organized into an expression of a magnetic field by placing a magnet under the piece of paper. Let the iron shavings represent matter, the material world; and let the magnetic energy simply represent energy.

One could, with some difficulty, "manually organize" the iron shavings into some arbitrary pattern. However, this arbitrary pattern would not be an expression of the magnetic energy. This is an "unconscious manipulation of nature." If one were conscious of the magnetic energy and simply allowed the iron shavings to align with this energy, we would have a "conscious participation in nature."

Presently, we humans are trying to manually organize our material world. This crude organization is based on arbitrary, ego-related patterns, i.e. dogmas. Often this manual organization of our material world is in conflict with the natural energy patterns at hand. Thus our struggle. We have but to search for and align with the energy world and our material world will then shape itself according to nature's own inscrutable ways, in perfect harmony with the unarguable phenomenon of the universe. We must explore the seemingly intangible world of energy. It is our new frontier. We must align with, i.e. join, this power to participate in our destiny - indeed, to even have a destiny.

Incident

I was lying in the tall grass under an apple tree in the field. Looking up through the tree branches at the scattered clouds in a late summer sky, I fell into a non-focused dream state. My eyes were open. The closest physical things to me were tree branches. The farthest things from me were the clouds. I began to feel energies between the tree branches and the clouds. These were haunting ghost-like energies of the past, present and future. There was really nothing to see visually. It was more like a telepathic observance. I was definitely "seeing" the activity of another dimension. Suddenly, a dart-like force shot through the non-visual telepathic picture. It was me! I saw myself in another dimension. There was no doubt. It was me. I remember my exact reaction. . . "Hey, that's me!"

I have found a dimension of intangibles. I have been "traveling" in it today. At times, I have become an intangible. Forces, or vibrations, or blankets of energy from the dimension of intangibles can be felt by the human being. There are vector-like forces. There are undulating vibrations. There are fog-like blankets. I believe these are aspects of consciousness that exist throughout the universe, but tend to harbor around specific masses or bodies in the "sky." It seems that all physical things are affected by and are a result of these forces in the dimension of intangibles. The first thing is to recognize it, then to explore it. Then to travel and dwell in it.

Once we realize that our simple dimension of life on material earth as humans can be escaped, it greatly reduces the security oriented importance of any "thing" in that dimension. It is my present opinion that all life forms on earth can receive or feel from the dimension of intangibles, whether they are aware of it or not. Look into these feelings. Follow them. You will see yourself and much, much more.

Energy - A Womb for Matter

Energy itself is like a void that matter is born into. It could be said that energy is a womb for matter. Modern physics tells us that matter can be converted into energy and energy into matter and that neither are ever really spent- they just move back and forth from one form to the other giving us the illusion of the disappearance of matter and the spending of energy. Thus there is a dance between energy and matter; a dance that, if we understood it, could give us a more whole view of our existence.

Human energy functions much the same as the energy explored in quantum physics. Energy is a potential- a void destined to be filled with whatever fits into the particular "shape" of the void. Human energy is shaped or organized in the world of mind. It is here that we create a potential or mold for a material world experience or "thing" to manifest in. These experiences and things born into the molds of our energies are sometimes unpleasant, such as the existing potential for disease or war. The nature of our social structure creates a void for poverty and starvation and crime. Our cities create voids for slums. Our way of life creates the potential for extinction.

We could consciously participate to some extent in what manifests itself in our material world by being more observant and recognizing the importance of the role of the world of energy, for it is here that our reality is conceived. Indeed, this world of energy is the birth place of all that exists in our world of matter. Matter simply fills voids of potentiality created in the world of energy. This world of energy is organized in the mind by consciousness. Consequently we must be aware of our organization of energy. We must understand it. We must know that what we are creating there manifests in a physical form in the world of matter.

The level or degree of consciousness we make available to mind greatly affects the way we organize energy.

Our normal practice is to deal with things only after they have manifested in the material world. In fact, the material world is only half the picture for us, just as "high tide" is only half the picture in the cycle of the tides. We have learned that the tide comes and goes. We have accepted this and anyone working or living near the oceans allows for this and uses it in the docking of boats, the building of structures, etc. We are not surprised or perplexed by the tide because we know the gravity of the moon swells our waters and thus creates the "coming and going" of it. Likewise, there is a coming and going of matter - a coming and going of reality - a wave so to speak. The nature of this wave is a result of energy - energy organized by consciousness. Organized energy is constantly manifesting the "wave of reality." *If conscious mind changes the nature of energy, the resulting wave of matter, i.e. the material world, is thus changed accordingly.*

Consciousness organizes energy and energy is a womb for the material world. The place for us to consciously participate in the evolution of our material world is, therefore, in the world of energy. Once we have organized energy, nature itself takes over and creates our material world for us; changes our material world for us; or destroys our material world for us. *What nature does simply depends on how we have consciously or unconsciously organized energy.*

We must learn to watch and to "tune" energy because the world of matter is simply a result of the world of energy. More attention must be given to the world of energy. The two worlds are not necessarily separate. They are more like inseparable mates. This pattern in itself is probably the origin of the yen and yang concept, the male and female concept, the positive and negative concept, etc.

An understanding of this dance between energy and material world manifestations could help us with disease, relationships, war and much, much more. We have explored our physical sphere, the earth, quite thoroughly. Let us give equal attention to the exploration of our energy sphere. Our energy is almost like a "magic marker" that draws a picture and "presto", nature itself makes the picture a reality. Our energy is like a womb in which our reality is born. We tend to treat disease and war and poverty and starvation only with material world "remedies." This is like taking aspirin for the headache that we get while beating ourselves in the head with a hammer. The source of the headache is the hammer. Aspirin will not stop the hammer. The source of our realities, whatever they may be, is our energy. *If we want to change our reality, we must change our energy.*

Before we can explore the arena of mutual participation, we must recognize the existence of something besides our material selves- that something is our energy. Our energy band will lead us to the arena. Here we can participate in our evolution by organizing our energy. A very basic example of two different organizations of energy and how they are used is as follows:

Vector Energy and Blanket Energy

Vector energy manipulates matter. Blanket energy changes or evolves matter. We are most familiar with vector energy. Vector energy is like an ice pick breaking up ice, thus manipulating it into smaller pieces while still remaining ice. Blanket energy is like heat melting ice, thus changing it or evolving it into water. More heat and the water changes or evolves into steam and so on. Blanket energy creates a "space" or "place" or a condition that matter conforms to, thus creating the evolution of matter.

For example: On this planet we know of energies that we call "love" and "healing." These are really just two different words for the same energy. We normally use these energies as vectors only, thus they become an "act" - "I will love you" or "I will heal you." Vector healing like vector loving is the use of individually directed and selected narrow focused "rays" (or vectors) of an energy that is so abundant it seems absurd to use it in this way. It's like using a flashlight on a sunny day because, for some reason (dogma) we are not aware of the sunlight.

Some humans in this dimension of dogmatic darkness can focus a ray of healing or loving energy on another in such a strong way that it can be felt. This is considered an awesome power or gift; a gift from the place where there is light. This place is available for all of us to dwell in. If one lives in the light, one doesn't need a flashlight. If one deals in blanket energy, one doesn't need vector energy.

Healing and loving used as blanket energies create a condition, to which resulting reality will simply conform. In this place, healing and loving simply *are*. They are not focused vectors. *They are.* Think of plants on the bottom of a lake. No one has to water them because water is *there*. Likewise, no one has to "heal" or "love" in a blanket of healing and loving energy because healing and loving are *there*.

If we dwell there in our thoughts, the material world will conform, just as matter conforms to prevailing energy such as heat. We will be in and of the healing and loving place and therefore constantly *being* healed and loved just as the plants on the bottom of the lake are constantly *being* watered. Wherever we go, healing and loving will be. This blanket energy remains like residue after "we" leave. It is accumulative. It sets "waves" in motion, thus we can shape our evolution.

We can *live* healing and loving. We can let all our realities materialize from this condition. We can accumulate a lake, a world of healing and loving energy. Eventually, no one would have to *be healed or loved* because healing and loving would *be*. The lake, the water, can *be* - so healing and loving can *be*. This is blanket energy. We can become it via the arena of mutual participation.

53

The Coyote

I was running deep into the mesa
    when I saw him cross my path
He turned his eyes toward mine
    as he lightly glided by
He did not change his pace nor his direction
Neither afraid nor offended
    he did not strike fear in me
Like a silent shadow thru the sage
    he touched me where I have no name
Surrendering all previous intentions to this moment,
    I let myself glide along behind him
    but a stone's throw from his path
He looked back, aware that I had
    shed my human program
Knowing that he was still not afraid
    I ran faster and caught up to him
    still a stone's throw from his path but running beside him
I saw how effortless he glided
I felt myself doing the same
Two creatures running on the mesa
We found a plane of mutual existence.

The Plane of Mutual Existence

A way to approach the arena of mutual participation in a two-dimensional abstract form is on the accompanying page. Call the lower "mass" nature macroworld diminishing to microworld- diminishing to subatomic world where matter has diminished to nothing more than a force field. Physicists are observing these days that a force field seems to be the bottom line of matter.

Call the upper "mass" humanity. Again macroworld, human swarm belief systems, diminishing to microworld, neural impulses in the brain. Neural impulses result in "thoughts" which themselves are a kind of force field. Both nature's force fields and humanities' force fields exist at a subatomic level in terms of relevant matter. Physicists are finding that with the input of energy, matter (particles) can simply "appear" in a force field. They have observed a dance between particles and force fields and they are not sure which comes from which. There is a place at the subatomic level where the force fields of nature and the force fields of human consciousness can co-mingle at a common "scale." This is the arena of mutual participation. The diagram opposite graphically illustrates the "tuning" necessary to reach this arena. We must be able to "tune" to a place where all things exist mutually, thus we are looking for a *plane of mutual existence.*

The accompanying diagram shows (abstractly) the units (quanta) of each mass diminishing into the other. There is one particular line where the units of the above are of the same magnitude as those of the below. It is in this place, where the quanta of two different worlds are of the same magnitude and same scale, that they can "hear" each other- they can exchange, communicate, merge. Just above this place on the diagram, the quanta from above are slightly larger than those from below and consequently they are too "loud" to be heard by the quanta from below. Thus there is no communication or union. Just below this place the lower quanta are slightly larger than those coming from above and again an imbalance of one mass or reality over the other and again no exchange or communication. However, the line where all the dots/quanta are the same is where real exchange of awareness between worlds can occur. This is where we can hear nature and nature can hear us. This is where we can become one with nature and the universe. It is a very delicate matter of tuning or balancing force fields (in this example- ours with nature's). In other places (above and below the plane of mutual existence) we can push nature around and/or nature can push us around; but where the quanta are in equilibrium, we merge and move as "one light", "one wave", "one pulse"- human/God/nature/cosmos.

Acute consciousness of the moment can help us "tune" to this place. It is the place where we are not talking louder than our brothers and sisters. It is the place where there is enough bread for everyone. It is the place where we take from the earth with one hand and give to the earth with the other. It is the place where animals breathe the breath of plants and plants breathe the breath of animals. It is a place of balance within and without. This "arena" is where we sing the song of life, where we work and live *through* the earth rather than just on it. In the arena, at the plane of mutual existence, we do not find good or evil for both are a sign of imbalance.

In the diagram, there is only one line of dots between the worlds that are all the same size. It is faint but therein lies all the power of both worlds. This plane of mutual existence is there between any two worlds; any two masses; any two humans; any two countries; and even between a man and his garbage. Here, all the answers to all the questions - all the solutions to all the problems will be as simple as water deciding which way to run down a mountain.

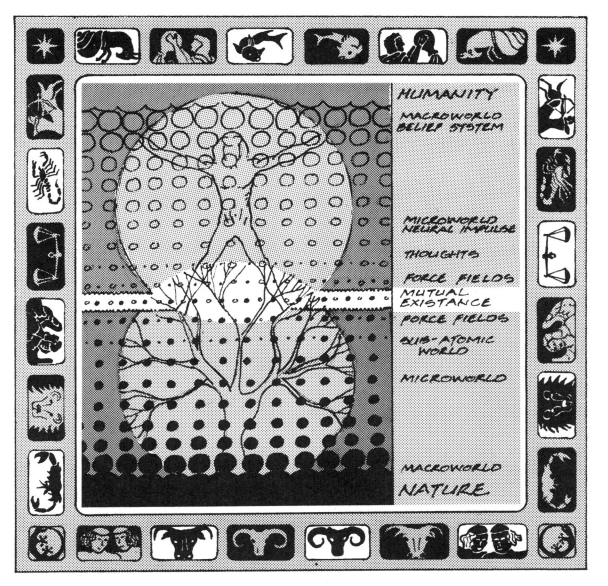

HUMANITY

MACROWORLD
BELIEF SYSTEM

MICROWORLD
NEURAL IMPULSE

THOUGHTS

FORCE FIELDS

MUTUAL
EXISTANCE

FORCE FIELDS

SUB-ATOMIC
WORLD

MICROWORLD

MACROWORLD
NATURE

Avenues Between Mind and Matter

In brain research, we have found that there is no "control" over certain motor activities. That is to say that once we decide to pick up a pen and write, the neurons of the brain take over and through their networks, activate the muscles. We do not have conscious control over the neuron to muscle network. We do not even fully understand how it works. "Will" is the power we have conscious control of. Execution of will takes place automatically within the body. This is very similar to the execution or manifestation of the material world brought about by the "will" of organized energy as previously discussed. This phenomenon is available to us on many levels. Presently, we laboriously execute our "wills" ourselves, at great expense to the planet and the quality of life.

I can't "will" the particular configuration of muscle contractions that come into play when I write my name. I can simply decide to write my name and let the act unfold according to its own inscrutable ways. Similarly, matter conforming to organized energy is an act that unfolds according to its own inscrutable ways. In learning to write my name I laboriously went through the physical rudiments, but now "will" is the only conscious activity associated with writing my name. The rest is automatic. I have organized my energy. Will is actually organized energy.

In the world outside our bodies, we are presently involved in the laborious activity of going through the physical rudiments of executing our wills. We have not yet found (or have lost) the avenues that allow acts to unfold according to their own inscrutable ways, i.e. we are not organizing energy, we are simply manipulating matter. For instance, most of us cannot "will" a rock to move. We have to pick it up and physically move it just as we have to physically and awkwardly move the pen in the crude configuration of our name at first. "Will", or organized energy, can be converted into specific movements the same way ice is turned into water by the organized energy called heat. It is simply a matter of organizing energy and being familiar with the natural effects of that organized energy.

In our current civilization, we act out specific movements as if just learning to write our name. We build a civilization rather than "willing" it through a fluid connection with the natural phenomenon.

"Avenues" between mind and matter exist in the arena of mutual participation. If we begin to "tune" to the plane of mutual existence between ourselves and other humans as well as between ourselves and other facets of nature, we are likely to find the beginnings of an avenue through which travels a fluid connection with natural phenomenon.

We could misuse this much worse than we are currently misusing our awkward ability to physically execute "will", i.e. manipulate matter. Consequently, the act of acquiring this power is synonymous with the act of acquiring appropriate consciousness so that we will not misuse the power. In other words, the degree of the expansion of consciousness required to achieve this is the same as that required to assure that we won't misuse it.

You can turn your staff into a serpent only when you are pure enough that the serpent won't bite you.

CHAPTER FOUR
THE COMING OF THE
WIZARDS

A Word About Magic

Real magic is neither a manipulation nor has power over anything. It is an alignment *with* power- the power of natural, unarguable phenomenon. Humans can achieve this alignment only by "stepping" out of dogma. Outside of dogma, mind executes another, far more fluid reality not subject to the limits of the human condition. This reality is available to what we call the subconscious.

The conscious is the hypnotic state of being, into which the swarm of humanity has evolved as a result of its "shell" of dogma. This shell is dense, limiting, and confining, and requires/allows only a shallow portion of mind to manifest. We call this shallow portion of mind conscious. Only when we are detached from dogma can we reach the deeper subconscious. It is the subconscious which deals in magic.

As a result of our introverted evolution (i.e. the fact that we live and grow within the confines of a shell of dogma), our attachment to this shallow portion of mind called conscious has developed to a greater degree than that of the deeper subconscious. In fact, the subconscious has been very much squelched these days. This is most unfortunate because the subconscious, not being subject to dogma, is rooted deeply in the very sources of our existence and is, therefore, *a reservoir of power*. What the subconscious wants, it gets. It is the subconscious that is capable of organizing energy. The conscious simply manipulates matter. However, the subconscious is not allowed to surface in our society except in dreams or what we call the "insane."

Insane - the state of not being sane
Sane - the state of mind of the majority
Voluntarily entering a state of "insanity" takes great strength and courage.

For us, magic is basically the art of allowing the subconscious to prevail over the conscious. I say art because those involved in magic who do not have it down to an art usually get locked up or crucified. *The "art" of magic weaves organized energy into the swarm of humanity in a way that can cause the swarm to evolve without being aware of it.* This allows the swarm access to "medicine" that is simply unacceptable to existing dogma which in turn brings about silent revolution and expanded evolution.

Magic is the uninhibited will of the subconscious. The subconscious is the "stage" for intuition. Intuition is the 'voice' of the energy band.

Behind the dense foliage of human knowledge lies the clearing of intuition

Naivete is an arrow that penetrates dogma.

I went insane
     'cause I had a lot of things I wanted to see
And as I went insane
     there was a coming of a new being inside of me

It didn't know of money
     and it didn't know of time
But it spoke in every language
     and it spoke in every sign

It's the wizard in my mind

This wizard is a leopard
     and it stalks inside my head
     like it was home
And it says it owns my shadow
     and it seems like I'll never be alone

It took my hand and took my heart
     and took my memory
And it took me to Uranus
     and it took me there to see . . .

The neon lights of Broadway
The screeching cars on the highway
The bleeding hearts on the byway
And the plastic cards and letters
     from the whole Universe.

The Coming of the Wizards
The wizards came as four entities in a pillar of fire.

It was late afternoon and I was lying in a pyramid on my back. I was relaxing and drifting. I remember a swirling purple and red misty haze began to fill my vision. There was a lot of turbulence. Out of the swirling mist a pillar of fire began to materialize. It burned and glowed stable and strong in the middle of the turbulent red and purple mist. On top of the pillar of fire I began to see four distinct colors of flame. Then a white glow began to appear in the middle of each color of flame. These white glows each began to emanate a "presence" first weak then getting stronger and stronger. At this point I knew "something" was happening, but it was so beautiful and exciting I forgot to be afraid. I knew the "presence" in the colored flames was four different entities. They all spoke to me in unison without words. The opposite message was communicated. Then they simply said they were wizards and each would speak to me individually. This experience was so vivid, beautiful and intense, that I have never even slightly questioned the validity of it nor the content of the messages. As a matter of fact, the message of the wizards is growing in validity with every day of my life. The following pages relay. . .

The Message of the Wizards.

"Believe in the pieces of
    magic you've found
Believe the intuitive voices
    that sound
Stand out side yourself
And channel your deeds
And you will have eyes
    that see
Forget all the dogma that
    rots in your brain
Close your eyes wide and
    they'll open again."

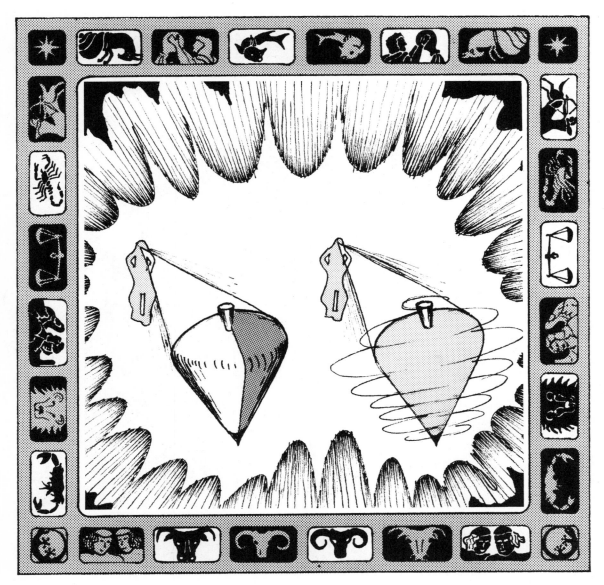

The First Wizard

The first wizard told me about time and motion and magic. It used the example of a toy top that spins. The top is painted two different colors. While the top is motionless, these two colors appear as two individual spaces on the surface of the top. When the top begins to spin, the two colors blend into one color. Time and motion took the two colors on the surface of the top and made them one.

The wizards, however, say that time and motion must be applied to the observer rather than what is being observed. In this respect time and motion not only change the vantage point- they create a situation where the vantage point is no longer a point but a line circling around the object being observed, i.e. *an orbit*. Consequently, what is being observed (be it abstract, conceptual, or physical) is much more thoroughly examined and finally much more fully understood.

Wizards have developed the ability to orbit - i.e. to maneuver. Fixed humans cannot maneuver. Their vision comes from a fixed position.

Learn to recognize and observe strength. . .

Then be it.

The Second Wizard

The second wizard told me about the application of maneuverability. An example involving violence was used.

Imagine you are driving in the wide open salt flats of Utah. Way in the distance you can see an obstacle. Because you can maneuver the car, you can obviously avoid it with little effort. This maneuverability and the fact that the wide openness of the salt flats allows you to see things long before you encounter them gives you complete control over what you do and do not encounter.

Violence in ones life span is as easy to deal with as the obstacle in the salt flats if one can "see" and "maneuver." This ability to "see" and "maneuver" in space and time (not just on the earth) must be developed.

Many people and groups of people are against violence. They do not have the vision nor the maneuverability to totally steer clear of it so they get to it and stop., Their energy is blocked by the obstacle. Often, people who believe in violence, smash right through the obstacle. This is usually damaging in some way (war for instance). If they could have seen the obstacle from a distance and were aware of their maneuverability in space and time, they could have made their way without ever encountering the obstacle.

Imagine how much maneuverability one has in the salt flats of Utah as compared to the usual ribbon of highway. The potential maneuverability in space and time as compared to living and dealing with time in sequence and space from one vantage point is infinitely more than this.

This is not a method of avoiding violence. It is a method of making violence non-existent in ones path. This is much easier said that done. It involves development of vision and maneuverability. This is turn involves development of self energy which comes from immaculate concentration.

No maneuverability is like being trapped on a highway.

One meets obstacles that block the way.

67

Maneuverability is like being on the salt flats. . .

The "way" is bigger than the obstacle.

The Third Wizard
The third wizard used another basic example for the explanation of maneuverability and introduced the use of distance.

Imagine standing in front of a huge building. A complicated building like an air terminal or a cathedral. You are almost consumed by the building as you look up, and to both sides and still can't see all of it. You could get lost in it. You have no feeling for what it is totally like. You can only see one elevation.

Now walk all the way around this building- once, twice, three, times. Each time you see and understand more. You now have a feeling for the nature and scope of the entire building.

Now imagine you could go up and over the top of the building - down the other side, into the ground and under the building and back up to where you started. Imagine all that you would see and absorb in doing this once, twice, three, times.

You now have the total exterior of the building inside your head as a result of your "orbiting" around it in two different orbits. The more different orbits you take and the more times you orbit, the better you understand the building and the more clearly it exists in your head.

Now apply distance to these orbits. The greater distance you are from the building in your orbit, the more you see in terms of how the building relates to what is around it and the more total picture you get of it. The closer you are to it in your orbit, the more detail you observe with respect to the building itself. Both orbits with respect to distance are enlightening in a different way.

Thus is the orbit of self observation and life observation for fixed humans. The threshold of cosmic travel awaits the development of maneuverability. Maneuverability is a specific organization of human energy.

"The Eastern way of thinking rather consists in a circling round the object of contemplation.

. . . a many-sided, i.e., multidimensional impression formed from the superimposition of single impressions from different points of view."

Lama Govinda

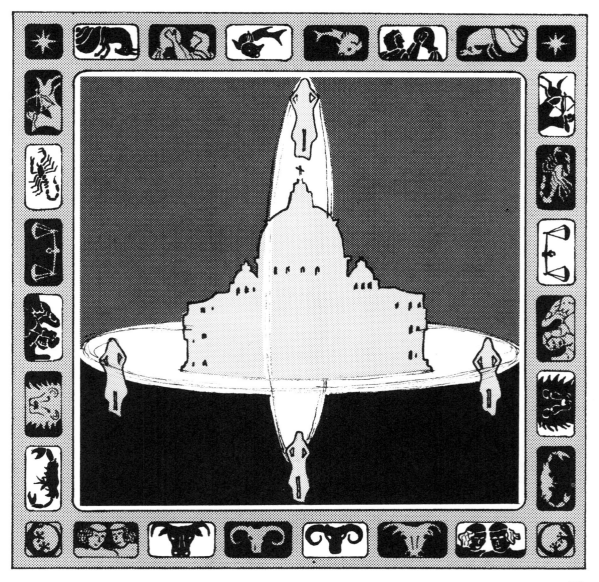

The Fourth Wizard (three years later)

I was asleep in a little dome I had made as a bedroom out on the mesa. (see opposite page). I woke up to notice a red light and with it a presence outside the dome. It seemed like a somewhat oppressive communication of some type. I was not afraid. I got out of bed, went outside and confronted it so directly that the presence and the light left.

I got back in bed. Very shortly I noticed a yellow light and a "presence" inside the dome. This time I experienced fear because both the light and the presence were more intense and they were right inside the dome with me. My heart began beating so fast it became like a buzzing motor in my chest. There was an intense buzzing in my head too. With the buzzing in my heart and in my head, and the yellow light, the fear became quite intense. I could, I found, overpower the fearful situation as it crescendoed. I considered waking my wife and telling her something was happening to me. The yellow light was concentrated before my eyes- not all over like the red one. In the center of the yellow light was a white glow. The white glow was the presence- a very strong presence.

It didn't occur to me at the time but this was very much like the wizard experience I had three years before where four wizards came but only three actually communicated with me. After three years I was communicating with the fourth wizard.

The heart buzzing, the buzzing sound in my head, the yellow light and presence all came and faded relative to the intensity of my fear. I remember thinking I must be having some kind of attack. The buzzing was simply overtaking my body. Just when I was ready to lose it, I got a grip on the situation enough to relate it to other similar past experiences. Then it occurred to me to rise above the fear. Fear had appeared to be a barrier in my past experiences. I remember saying to myself "go with it- go with it." I did. The fear was gone. Everything, the buzzing in my heart and head, the light, and the presence increased to an intensity that I wouldn't allow before. I was totally going for it. There was no turning back. Then, in the middle of the white glow inside the yellow light, the image of a face came. It materialized and changed until it became quite clear. I received a message without words from the image. The message was something like "ok, now that I have reached you, I'll be back." Then everything was gone. I slept.

I realized later this was the fourth wizard. My choice to dissolve fear made the message of the fourth wizard available to me. For the next several months I wrote and drew diagrams almost automatically. This material is presented on the following pages.

Fear is a barrier
beyond which lies eternity.

Any time things get too weird
    I pretend I just arrived
on the scene.

This gives me no reference
    for fear.

THE FOURTH WIZARD HAS SPOKEN:
IT WAITED THREE YEARS AFTER THE OTHERS.

ONE'S STAGE OF GROWTH HAS TO CORRELATE WITH THE INFORMATION ONE RECEIVES. THE INFORMATION IS THERE ALL THE TIME. ONE SIMPLY HAS TO GROW STRONG ENOUGH TO "CLIMB" HIGH ENOUGH OUT OF DOGMA, FEAR, ETC. TO SEE IT. THE HIGHER YOU GO IN OUR LIMITED PHYSICAL REALITY, THE FARTHER YOU CAN SEE. CONSIDER YOURSELF A HOT AIR BALLOON. NOW CUT THE ROPES OF FEAR AND DOGMA THAT ANCHOR YOU TO THE GROUND. RELEASE AND RELAX- NO EFFORT. NATURE WILL TAKE YOU TO THE HEIGHTS FROM WHICH YOU CAN "SEE", BUT *YOU* MUST CUT THE ROPES.

THE FOURTH WIZARD REVEALED TWO THINGS:
SPHERICAL VISION
THE NATURE OF WIZARDS

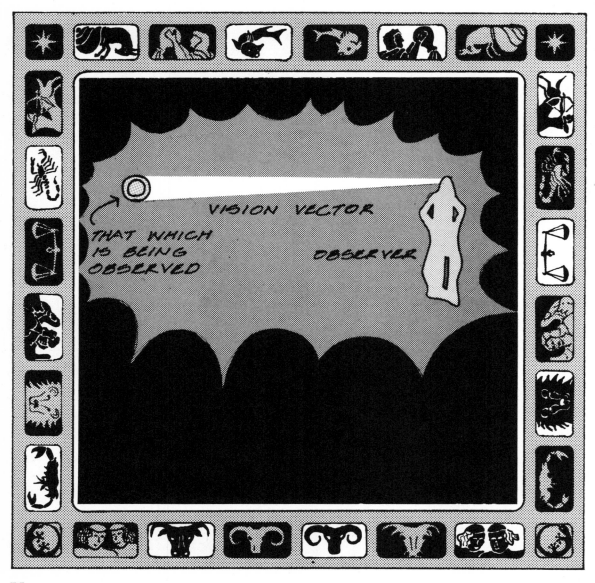

Spherical Vision

The type of physical vision we are accustomed to using could be called vector vision- a line or ray of interaction involving both magnitude and direction. The magnitude of the vision vector relates to how much of the observer's attention is focused on that which is being observed. There is both an observation and a "creation" going on simultaneously in this interaction.

If the observer can maneuver in a single simple orbit, the observation, or awareness, attains dimension. The line of interaction becomes a *field* of interaction. The connection between the observer and that which is being observed is obviously much greater here.

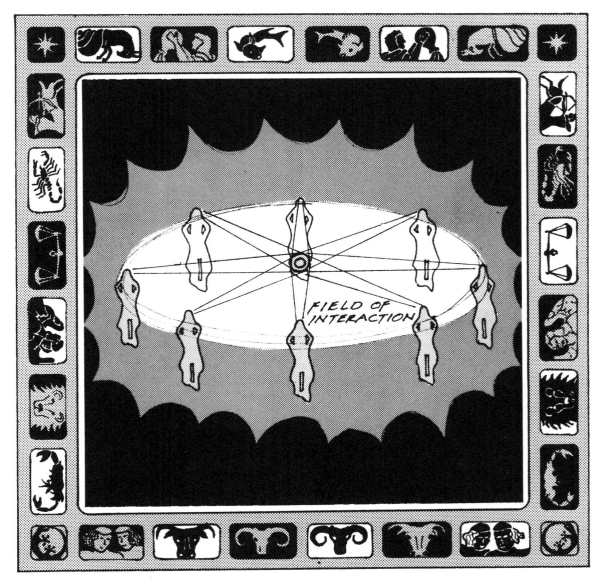

FIELD OF INTERACTION

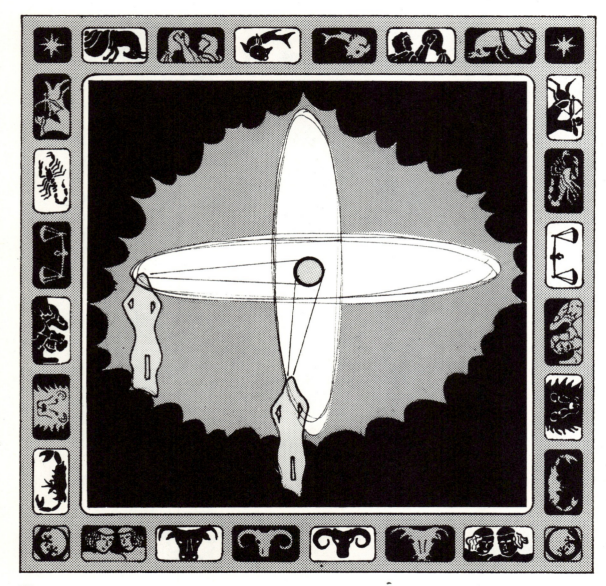

Now consider the added dimension of two orbits.

Consider four orbits.

The interaction between the observer and that which is being observed is

a system.

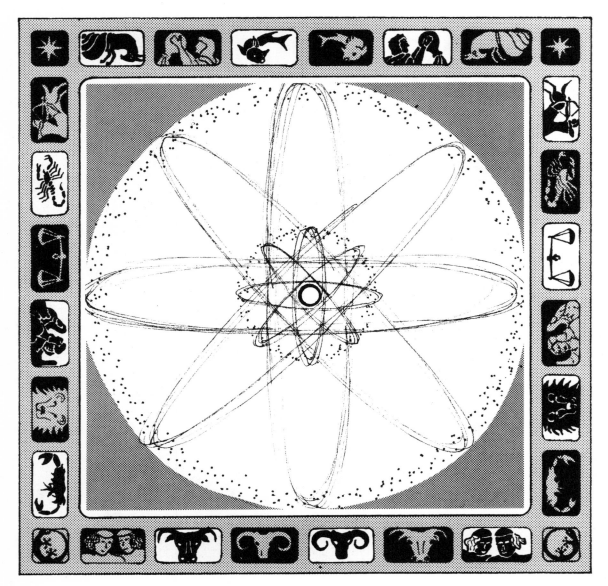

Consider eight orbits - four close and four distant

Notice the spheres being formed by the orbits. An infinite number of orbits around that which is being observed results in a sphere being formed around the object. Likewise, an infinite number of spheres will be possible due to the varying distances from the object.

A graphic analogy of the result is a gaseous sphere around the object being observed- every "particle" of which is the "eye of the observer." (See opposite page).

THIS IS THE BASIC CONCEPT OF
SPHERICAL VISION.

THROUGH THIS PROCESS, VISION
BECOMES INTERACTION.

INTERACTION IS THE PULSE OF
THE UNIVERSE.

EXPANDED INTERACTION RESULTS
IN A *NON-LOCAL* TYPE OF AWARE-
NESS.

WE ARE TALKING ABOUT COSMIC
TRAVEL; INTO A ROCK; INTO THE
BODY OF A BIRD; INTO THE MIND
OF A HUMAN; INTO THE DEPTHS. .

OF THE UNIVERSE.

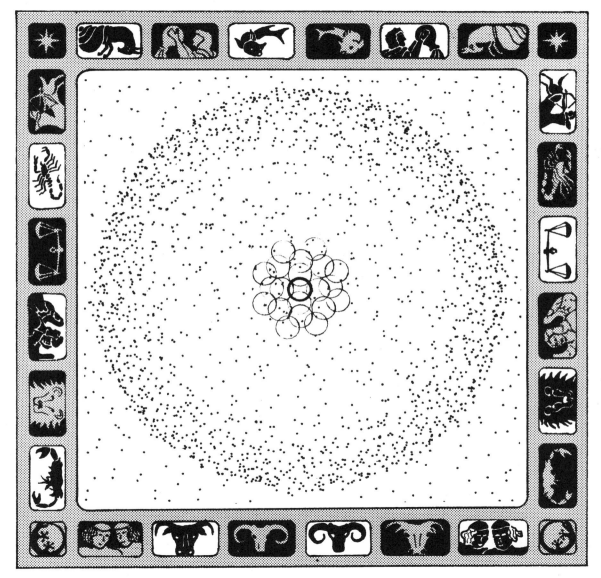

The Nature of Wizards

Wizards are a link between human dogma and unarguable phenomenon. Another way of saying this is wizards are a link between "us" and raw energy, the us and the US. They can exist in our dogmas (our realities) with us and actually be us with us. They can also be raw energy unhampered by human dogma. They have mastered spherical vision to the point of interaction with unarguable phenomenon.

The ability of wizards to interact with both us and unarguable phenomenon makes them a link between us and raw energy. Through interaction with us, they stretch/expand/awaken/excite us. They are the force that causes the baby chick to begin breaking out of the egg. They excite us to the point of breaking out of our "egg" and evolving in step with the processes of our planet. Our planet doesn't have a dogma, so it evolves with the processes of our solar system, without resistance. Our solar system evolves with the processes of the universe which are simply the patterns of raw energy. Evolution, a continuous "breaking out of one reality into another" process, is our available path toward raw energy. Wizards are a force behind evolution.

We tend to get trapped by our dogmas in a three-dimensional reality governed by a linear concept of time. Wizards can come there with us to a particular reality but they also can "travel" back and forth between all realities as well as between all realities and raw energy. For a normalized human to become a wizard, he/she must *denormalize*. Denormalization occurs naturally when one totally surrenders to ones energy band. Find it, learn to recognize it and be it. It is like finding the real current in a river as opposed to drifting in the still, sometimes stagnate, waters which are part of the river but not part of the real current. There is much more power in the real current. Likewise, there is much more power in ones energy band. With this power from the energy band, one can break out of dogma and learn to maneuver and ultimately master the concept of spherical vision. Then interaction with unarguable phenomenon, and finally raw energy, is possible.

Early maneuvering is only from one reality to another like a baby first walking from a chair to a couch. Later maneuvering takes place in the "matrix" (see diagram) between realities. This matrix is the soup of which all realities are a part. Realities are eddies in the current of the universe. The current of the universe is this matrix. This is where unarguable phenomenon come from, and it is actually where raw energy can be touched or interacted with. It is like the arena of mutual participation of all realities. This matrix is without image or dogma. It is the "place", or anti-place, where raw energy dances the dance of the universe without human limitations. It is beyond light. It is angel consciousness. We separate ourselves from this matrix and call our separateness reality.

Realities are simply "our" own separations from raw energy. They exist only as long as we use them to separate us from all that is and is not. Unarguable phenomenon from the matrix penetrate our realities. (like the arrows penetrating circles in the diagram opposite).But we still maintain a separation from these phenomenon much the way a chick in an egg is separate from the "outside world." We can maneuver outside the "egg" with the help of the wizard energy.

EVENTUALLY, MANEUVERING WILL CEASE TO BE NECESSARY AS THE MANEUVERING ENTITY REALIZES ITS ABILITY TO MERGE WITH THE MATRIX. IT IS AT THIS POINT THAT NON-LOCAL AWARENESS, (A KIND OF TOTAL AWARENESS AND UNITY OF ALL) BEGINS TO PREVAIL. AT THIS POINT, WIZARDS CEASE TO EXIST. **_WHAT KEEPS US SEPARATE IS THAT WE ARE AFRAID TO "CEASE TO EXIST."_**

THIS DIAGRAM ILLUSTRATES VARIOUS REALITIES FROM DIFFERENT TIMES AND DOGMAS ALL GOING ON AT ONCE IN THE MATRIX. THESE REALITIES ARE PENETRATED BY VARIOUS UNARGUEABLE PHENOMENON AND WIZARD ENERGY FROM THE MATRIX. WIZARDS "TRAVEL" WITHIN, THROUGH, AND BETWEEN REALITIES VIA THE MATRIX. NORMALIZED HUMANS CAN ONLY TRAVEL _WITHIN_ A REALITY.

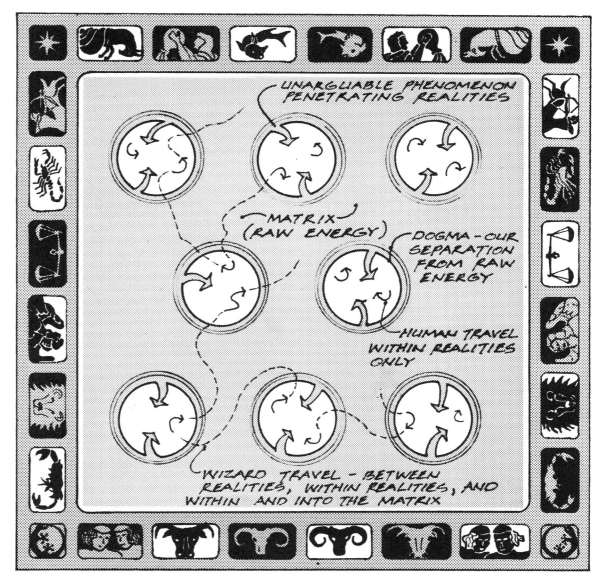

UNARGUABLE PHENOMENON PENETRATING REALITIES

MATRIX (RAW ENERGY)

DOGMA - OUR SEPARATION FROM RAW ENERGY

HUMAN TRAVEL WITHIN REALITIES ONLY

WIZARD TRAVEL - BETWEEN REALITIES, WITHIN REALITIES, AND WITHIN AND INTO THE MATRIX

Wizards can maneuver, function, dwell and exist in all reality zones, or they can cease to exist in the matrix. *Existence is only a relevant state within a reality.* It has no meaning in the matrix. The ability of wizards to maneuver can be understood by observing an unarguable phenomenon from nature. Observe water, a mixture of hydrogen and oxygen. Observe air, a mixture of nitrogen and oxygen. Oxygen is the common denominator of the two. It exists in both. Wizards are a common denominator between realities and the matrix and thus can exist, or cease to exist, in both. Oxygen moves back and forth between air and water thru evaporation and condensation. In a similar way wizards move back and forth between realities and the matrix. There is much symbology in nature to reveal to us that we are but a form that raw energy has taken and it is our dogmas that keep us *only* in this form.

There is the possibility of learning to maneuver away from this form thereby using it only as a "home base," rather than an absolute and only form. The unarguable phenomenon of union (marriage, mating, relationship, etc. in the human dogma) is an opportunity and an inspiration for us to begin the journey away from our own individual absolute form. Physically, mating illustrates a process that results in two merging to make one. This one is both, yet neither. In mating we leave the individual form, surrender, let go, for an instant, just long enough to conceive. Then it's back to home base, our *individual* selves. There is much trauma here emotionally, as the merger of bodies happens, but the merger of egos rarely happens. Physically, a being is born that is part of both, but the original two egos return to home base unable to journey from the form. *Egos are not road-worthy for maneuvering between realities.*

As a baby grows to be a child, it is carried, without choice, by nature from one reality to another (baby to child). As a child grows into an adult, it is carried, without choice, by nature from one reality to another (child to adult). As an adult grows or shall we say if an adult is to grow, it is *by choice*. At this point nature no longer carries us. The point of choice is where we begin to be a conscious force in our own evolution. Therefore, if an adult attempts union and is afraid to maneuver away from the ego "form", there is tension. The dogma of an individual adult won't work for a union. A baby ceases to exist when it becomes a child. A child ceases to exist when it becomes an adult. The individual adult too must cease to exist to experience union. The process of taking a mate is an opportunity to continue growth - to learn to maneuver by choice from one reality to another. Thus, the various physical and emotional attractions of the mating situation are unarguable phenomenon from which we can learn maneuverability. They lure us into a dynamic situation where one learns to maneuver or one suffers. *Suffering is not necessary, maneuvering is.* Learning to maneuver from the ego will result in "travel" between realities. This kind of travel can acquaint one with the art of ceasing to exist which is the only way to enter the matrix.

Ceasing to exist means doing away with the "home base." Wizards are unattached to any home base or reality. They are free bodies. They can flow from one reality into another. They do not need "cooperation" so to speak from the other reality. If a wizard were to become red paint and consciously flow into yellow paint, the result would be orange paint. The yellow paint did not have to consciously participate in the change or evolution of orange paint. A true wizard could merge with you and all you would know is that you are different. *Wizards bring about evolution of static realities through their lack of attachment to any reality.*

THE STRONG FORCES OF THE
UNARGUABLE PHENOMENON WE
CALL MATING BOTH IMPEL AND
INSPIRE US TO LEARN THE NATURE
OF THE WIZARD- TO LET GO OF
ONE REALITY AND FLOW INTO
ANOTHER NOT ONLY BECOMING,
BUT ALSO EVOLVING AND CHANG-
ING THAT REALITY. THROUGH THE
VOCABULARY OF OUR DOGMA,
THE UNIVERSE (VIA MATING) EN-
COURAGES US TO LEARN WHAT
WE MUST.

ISOLATE TWO REALITIES. CALL
ONE MAN AND ONE WOMAN.
NATURE PULLS THEM CLOSE AND
IMPELS THEM TO LEARN TO
MANEUVER TO AND FROM EACH
OTHER. THEY MERGE OR FLOW
INTO EACH OTHER AS WIZARDS,
BOTH CHANGING/EVOLVING ONE
ANOTHER. . . A UNION. IN THIS
DIAGRAM, THE DISC JUST BEFORE
THE "WHOLE" ILLUSTRATES BOTH
REALITIES AS INDIVIDUAL PARTS
OF A SINGLE DOGMA. AN AL-
CHEMY, A TRANSFORMATION TO
WHOLENESS, TAKES PLACE WHEN
EGOS CEASE TO EXIST. THIS IS A
RESULT OF TIME AND MOTION, i.e.
MANEUVERABILITY (LIKE THE
MESSAGE OF THE FIRST WIZARD
ON PAGE 63). WHOLENESS BEGINS
TO SHATTER DOGMA THUS AL-
LOWING US PASSAGE TO THE
MATRIX, TO THE UNIVERSE, AND
TO GOD.

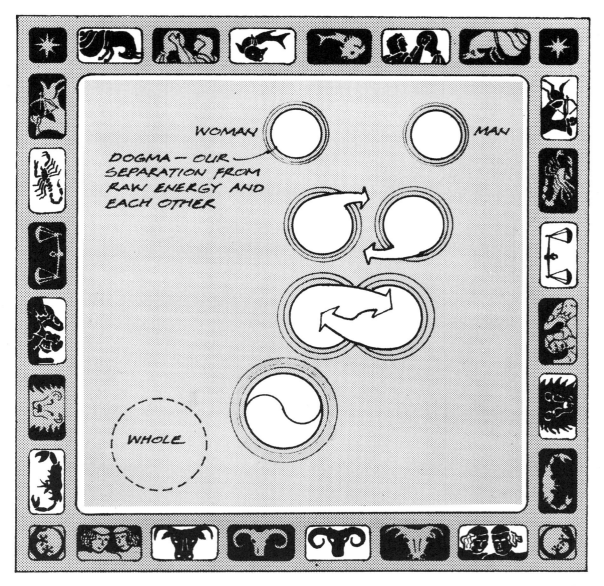

WOMAN

MAN

DOGMA — OUR
SEPARATION FROM
RAW ENERGY AND
EACH OTHER

WHOLE

A potential of relationship
    is learning to venture from
    the form.

Vanish from thyself.

This flowing into one another that can occur in a union between a male and a female, or any two individuals or entities, should not be confused with losing oneself in a relationship. Losing oneself is being a victim of the gravity of the other - like the earth's gravity pulls in a meteorite that crashes to the surface of the planet. Consciously and willfully venturing out of self into another under ones own "power"; knowing and accepting the alchemic change or evolution that will take place in both, is more like the previous example of oxygen moving from air to water. Oxygen is a significant aspect of both realities - air and water. It can actually become one or the other as a result of its ability to interact or unite with other atoms.

With respect to the human form, this ability to unite with others is a journey out of self and into others. It is a matter of breaking down barriers and out of dogmas. When we learn to leave self, we actually can learn to perceive thru the senses of others by interaction and familiarity with them. There is actually . . .your ear, his/her ear, and the collective ear. *Every sound can be heard by many ears.* Interaction broadens perception. There is specific interaction, (marriage relationship, etc.,) and non-specific interaction. Non-specific interaction is like a cosmic wind that constantly erodes barriers and dogmas. Non-specific interactions can be approached as follows:

What you see in yourself, accept in others
What you do best, share with others
What you can't do without, give to others
Alchemy begins.

The journey out of self is touched upon by many visions, concepts and religions in the human dogma; touched upon but rarely realized. There is an intuitive illusive desire for us all to be one. Thus our inherent unity shines through our dogma via intuition. The illusion of separateness brought about by our realities and dogmas is lessened as we learn to journey out of self and into another, both as individuals and as collective bodies such as races, countries, etc. Specific and non-specific interaction are the beginning of the journey from reality to reality.

The journey from reality to reality is the beginning of maneuvering. This is also where we really start learning to let go. Once one can easily let go of self and one reality to interact fully with another, the ice is broken on learning to let go. This letting go process reduces the attachment to any *one* reality thus making it easier to make the leap into letting go of the concept of reality altogether, (ceasing to exist). This is the journey into the matrix - merging with the matrix.

It sounds a lot like our physical process of death. Out bodies begin decomposing, letting go, from the time of birth until they are totally decomposed back into the earth after death. We are slowly letting go of our bodies without much awareness of it. This is happening regardless of choice. The journey to the matrix is happening regardless of whether we accept it or not. The nature of wizards is simply *to learn to die before we die.* That is, to consciously participate in, or ride, as in riding waves, unarguable phenomenon as opposed to thinking we are victims of them.

Death is truly an unarguable phenomenon or pattern in the universe. It is the nature of wizards to learn to recognize universal patterns and then surrender to or "ride" these patterns. Fighting or resisting these patterns is like resisting death. Resisting death just makes you miserable while you are alive. Imagine the difference between riding the waves of the ocean as opposed to resisting them. We cannot resist the patterns of the universe; therefore, we must join them and ride them. Our problem as humans, is that we don't even recognize most of them, so we find ourselves often trying to paddle up stream, caught in an impossibly strong current simply because *we aren't even aware that paddling downstream is an option.*

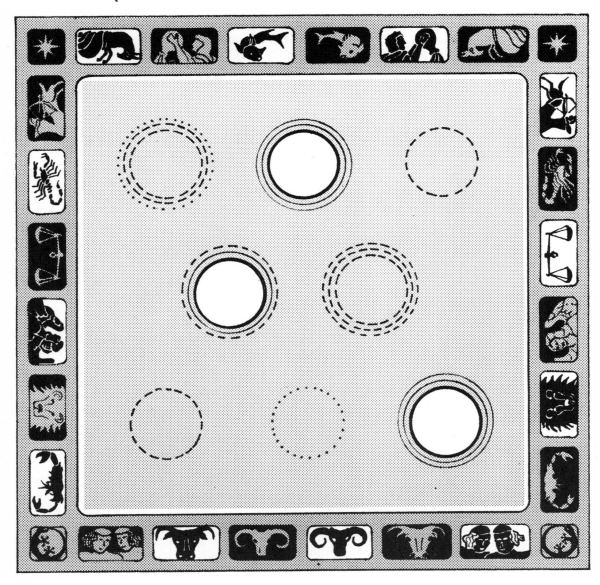

THIS DIAGRAM ILLUSTRATES SOME REALITIES DECOMPOSING INTO THE MATRIX. THIS IS HAPPENING WITHOUT CHOICE VIA DEATH. THIS PHENOMENON CAN ALSO HAPPEN *BY* CHOICE VIA CONSCIOUSNESS. WE ARE BASICALLY LOOKING AT A SITUATION VERY SIMILAR TO THE PREVIOUS ANALOGY OF OXYGEN MOVING BETWEEN AIR AND WATER. ***WE SEE THE EVAPORATION AND CONDENSATION OF REALITIES.*** THIS IS A PATTERN OF THE UNIVERSE. IF WE SURRENDER TO, AND RIDE THIS PATTERN WE WILL COME TO THE "PLACE" WHERE DEATH AND BIRTH MEET AND WE WILL LEARN TO DIE BEFORE WE DIE. WE WILL VENTURE INTO THE MATRIX KNOWING THE MATRIX CONDENSES INTO REALITIES OF WHICH WE WILL BE A PART; BUT OUR AWARENESS OF THE PATTERN OF EVAPORATION AND CONDENSATION OF REALITIES WILL KEEP THESE REALITIES AND THEIR EVENTUAL EVAPORATION IN A PROPER PERSPECTIVE. THUS WE CAN RIDE THE "WAVES" OF THE UNIVERSE. THIS IS THE NATURE OF WIZARDS.

Riding Universal Energy Patterns

A growing baby practices walking in the living room at home to gain the confidence necessary to walk in the outside world as an adult. Likewise, evolving adult humans can practice riding universal energy patterns in our immediate reality to gain the confidence necessary to venture into other realities, the universe at large and eventually the matrix itself. Just as walking is an eventual method of maneuvering for the baby, energy riding is an eventual method of maneuvering for the human adult.

Our reality, or dogma, is simply our egg or incubation chamber. In it, we develop ourselves through relating to the phenomenon (energies) at hand. When we learn to ride these energies, we are ready to "hatch" out of our egg and maneuver around the universe. We do not want to make a "career" of life in the egg lest our dogma and our one reality become crystalized. *Can an eagle arrive at its full potential in the egg?*

If we look at some very basic patterns of energy on our planet, (our egg) such as wind, light, and electricity we can see similarities. They are all unargueable phenomena. These similarities suggest certain universal patterns regarding energy. If we become aware of these patterns and learn to ride them, we gain the confidence to "ride" energy outside of our "egg." However, we seem to have a tendency to want to ride around in our egg forever. *Are we afraid to be born into our full potential?*

We are very pleased with ourselves, but we are not the ultimate evolution. With regard to this fact, *humility might just be the spark of continued growth,* i.e., the spark of conscious evolution itself. Wizards have a certain humility with regard to the patterns of the universe. This humility gives them the perspective they need to be free bodies capable of riding energy patterns.

We humans are in fact already riding energy and have been for years. Sail boats align themselves to a natural phenomenon, the wind, and move across the waters. River rafts ride moving currents. Skiers ride gravity, etc.

We are very familiar with the wind, so we will use it to outline some techniques for riding energy. It is interesting to note that we have used the phrase "harnessing energy" to describe some of our early steps as a civilization into this realm. Harnessing energy suggests that we have control *over* the natural phenomenon and puts us in the wrong state of mind (certainly not humility) for realizing the full potential of the situation. Again, *humility is one of the secrets of the wizards.*

Early in our development, energies such as the wind controlled us, scared us and literally pushed us around. Now, our little egos may need to feel they are in control for awhile. However, the way to ride energy to its full potential is to know the nature of the energy, so that it doesn't control or harm us, and to also realize that we can't control it. We are talking about an alignment, or a union, or a merging with energy. This is the way of the wizard. *Control is the way of the ego.*

RESISTANCE

THE FOLLOWING DIAGRAMS ILL-
USTRATE FOUR WAYS WE CAN RE-
LATE TO THE WIND. FIGURE ONE
SHOWS A FORM OF SHELTER RE-
SULTING IN PROTECTION FROM
THE WIND OR *RESISTANCE.*

ACCEPTANCE

FIGURE TWO SHOWS A FORM OF RECEPTION OR *ACCEPTANCE* WHICH RESULTS IN MOBILITY... LITERALLY RIDING THE WIND.

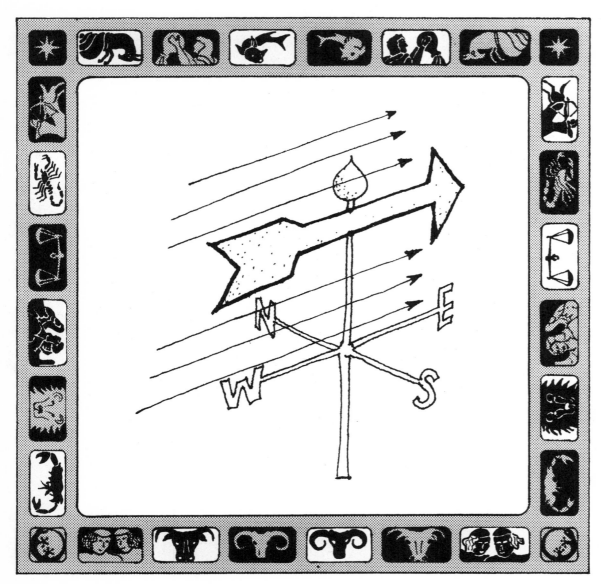

ALIGNMENT

FIGURE THREE ILLUSTRATES A TECHNIQUE OF UNIFICATION OR *ALIGNMENT.* WE USE THIS TO TELL US THE DIRECTION OF THE WIND. THIS PARTICULAR WAY OF RE-LATING TO THE WIND MINIMIZES THE EFFECT OF THE WIND ON THE BODY IN QUESTION.

TRANSFORMATION

FIGURE FOUR ILLUSTRATES A METHOD OF ENCOUNTERING THE WIND WHICH RESULTS IN A *TRANSFORMATION* OF WIND ENERGY.

Thus we have four ways of relating to the wind:

Resistance
Acceptance
Alignment
Transformation

Resistance is basically avoidance- not allowing any real interaction or encounter. It is the way of humans. Acceptance, alignment, and transformation are methods of energy encounter. They are the way of the wizard.

When we apply these four ways of relating to other familiar forms of energy, such as moving water, electricity, heat, light, etc., we find them to work in a similar way. There are certain forms of energy that we do not understand as well as others. Moving water for instance, is more commonly understood than light. However, if we accept the fact that all energy speaks the same language, we can relate to a particular form of energy and eventually ride it whether we understand it scientifically or not. As a matter of fact, learning to ride energy can help us arrive at a better scientific understanding of it. The point here is, *there are universal patterns regarding the nature of energy*. There are also many forms of energy that we, as yet, have not recognized as such. Resistance, acceptance, alignment and transformation are methods of relating to these patterns. Through these methods we can ride both familiar and unfamiliar forms of energy.

We have thus established a "key" for relating to energy patterns. Since the entire universe is matter and/or energy, and one can be converted to the other ($E=MC^2$), we find ourselves with a key to the entire universe. As the baby masters walking in the living room so that he/she may someday walk in the outside world, we can master riding energy forms within our reality, (our living-room, our egg) so that we may eventually "ride" around the universe with consciousness.

Let's explore the use of this key on a more local level- ourselves. We are energy. The massive force of the swarm of humanity can be related to with the four-sided key, i.e., it can be ridden. We do not have to be a victim of the movement of the swarm nor can we control it, but we can *ride it.* This would provide humankind with a much needed maneuverability within their reality and consequently facilitate conscious evolution. It is our inability to appropriately relate to the tremendous collective force of ourselves as a whole that makes for a narrow, inward spiraling, introverted evolution of humanity.

Let's take a single person, an outlaw, through the four methods of relating to energy - the energy of the swarm of humanity.

First, the outlaw *resists* the law as defined by the collective ideals of humankind. He must shelter himself and hide (like fig. one on the previous page) because he is vastly outnumbered and overpowered just as one person is vastly overpowered by a strong wind or raging river. Shelter from the swarm and hiding are his only options as long as resistance is his only method.

Now let's say, in order to gain mobility, he *accepts* the law as an existing form of energy. He then *aligns* with it by disguising himself as a law abiding citizen. This allows him to thoroughly encounter it and affords him a chance to *transform* it and use it to his advantage much like the windmill transforms the wind energy. Many corporate entities and politicians have already caught on to this and have been riding the swarm of humanity for years.

"Harnessing" humanity has failed many times in history, as we have seen with slavery, dictatorships, sex and class chauvinisms, etc. However, *riding* the collective energy of humanity is currently the most successful technique used by the "great exploiters" such as corporations and politicians, for the manipulation of the masses. While the politicians and corporations are using these methods in a very narrow, short-sighted, and egomanic way; their obvious success, which is evidenced by the mindless sheep-like following of millions of people, illustrates in a tangible way the potential of the principles of riding energy.

In order to ride any kind of energy to any place other than a "dead end", one must employ *spherical vision*. An energy rider simply ends up a politician or a guru without the guidance of spherical vision. The one who rides human energy with spherical vision *becomes an energy that everyone feels but no one votes for or worships*. This facilitates a conscious evolution of the unconscious and is the way of the wizard. The wizard encounters and rides the tremendous energy of the blossoming consciousness of humanity, thus bringing about its own and humanities' growth and evolution. The surfer rides *on* the wave - *the wizard rides in it.*

All of the devices used by the outlaw in the above analogy were used so he would no longer be at the mercy of the law. With the appropriate perspective gained by spherical vision, all these devices can be used by us as individuals, so we need no longer be at the mercy of the swarm of humanity, the elements, the government, the Russians, the Americans, ourselves, etc. All natural energy forms including humanity itself can be ridden. However, without spherical vision, the ride usually takes one right off the cliff of extinction. The development of spherical vision should occur simultaneously with the development of energy riding, just as the ability to steer an automobile must be developed simultaneously with the ability to accelerate through the gears.

These methods of energy riding can also be used to ride our own individual energies such as anger, happiness, fear, etc. This particular use is already covered in many books on self development. It is usually called "turning energy" and the concept has been beautifully presented many times over. The point is that our emotions too are energy - energy that we consciously or unconsciously organize prior to our actually experiencing it. We can resist these energies, as we often do, or we can accept, align with and transform them. For example, anger can be *transformed* into chopping wood or some other chore; happiness can be *transformed* into making a good soup; fear can be *aligned* with and used to penetrate through dogma to a greater awareness; and death can be *accepted* as a "way" of life.

To know real strength and power
    is to know the fragile space they come from
To have rein on flowing, limitless energy
    is to be reined by a wisdom not your own
To ride the awesome chariot
    that travels through dimensions and time
    and through the souls of men
    is to be ridden by the very awareness
    of all that lies within
To gather all momentum
    and reach unyielding speed
    is to leave the sky and labor
    in a world that you don't need
Weave thru this world a magic thread
    that sings a silent song
And the world will sing it too
    and you will then be gone.

Individual humans are energy. Humanity as a whole is energy. Natural phenomenon is energy. We exist as energy in a world of energy. Why not then communicate in the "native tongue" just as one who lives in Italy communicates in Italian?

Spherical vision results in an interaction- an encounter. This kind of encounter with the natural phenomena of our planet is an approach to using the "native tongue" of the earth. Through this encounter we can satisfy all the physical emotional, and spiritual "thirsts" of the human form. We can simply "drink" straight from the limitless flowing "streams," "rivers" and "seas" of energy all around us. It is dogma, our separation from raw energy, that keeps us from taking this drink.

As a result of this separation, resistance is most often the way we relate to natural phenomena. We seem to expend most of the earth's and our own physical energy protecting ourselves from (resisting) the sun, the wind, other elements, each other and all else. Through the nature of wizards we can learn the art of direct energy encounter with respect to all forms of energy- including ourselves.

When we encounter energy directly, a transformation takes place. We transform energy and energy transforms us. This is similar to the union between man and woman discussed earlier. We are talking about a union, an alchemy, of two forms of energy. This can be person to person, person to earth or person to universe. This alchemy is a method of riding energy.

Developing a rapport with and riding natural energy could save us the trauma of physically mining the earth and emotionally and spiritually mining ourselves to manufacture a "synthetic" energy. We presently use this synthetic energy to shelter us from (to resist) the very natural energy we could be riding.

We are destroying ourselves and our planet in the process of making energy when there is infinitely more than enough existing within and around us to do everything physically, mentally and spiritually that we could ever dream of. Direct encounter of universal energy patterns is a method of learning to walk here in the "living room", our earth, before we venture into the "outside world"; the universe, the matrix. This method is tangibly applied with respect to our present day to day life through the techniques of "direct living" outlined in the next chapter. We can learn through slowly leaning into direct living, to exist in harmony with the earth. We can bring about an alchemy between ourselves and the earth and learn to "ride" the earth rather than exploit it at the price of eventual destruction of ourselves.

Our success at riding the energy patterns of the earth will give us the confidence and the ability to ride universal energy patterns that go beyond our material reality and beyond "life" as we know it. There are energy patterns, (unarguable phenomenon) in our own reality that we must learn to ride in order to continue to exist in that reality. Direct living is an immediate, tangible approach to this energy riding and the ways of the wizard can facilitate it. Direct living can place us in a position and state of mind from which we can learn to ride energy patterns that are not even available to us in our present condition. It is these patterns that will take us into other realities, the universe and the matrix, i.e. home to God. If we consciously choose to do this, we have chosen "everlasting life" and we will "dwell in the house of the Lord forever."[1]

[1] 23rd Psalm

If a mountain stream
    had an ego,
It might never make it
    to the ocean.

CHAPTER FIVE
DIRECT LIVING

We Are The Earth

There has been talk of being detached from our physical surroundings - that maybe it is more "spiritual" to be less attached to the physical plane. This type of thinking has exposed the planet we live on to neglect and abuse by humanity.

How can we be enlightened beings on an abused planet?

We are born out of, sustained by, and received back into this planet. We *are* this planet- we *are* the earth. The more we surrender to this unarguable phenomenon (that we are not separate from the earth), the more natural power we will derive from our environment. We cannot fully realize our power, our potential, until we realize it is coming through the earth to us, just as life comes to an apple through a tree. Can the apple grow without the tree? Can humanity grow without the earth? If we relate to the earth as if it were our own body (as it really is), not only will our priorities and our way of life change, *but so will the scope of our power.* The earth itself is the "wave" of energy we must learn to ride. If a surfer appropriately relates to a wave, his ride is like a brief moment of ecstasy. If he does not appropriately relate to the wave, he is in for what could be a brief moment of hell. Likewise, if humanity appropriately relates to the earth, our "ride", our life, will be like a brief moment of ecstasy. If we do not appropriately relate to the earth, we are in for what could be a brief moment of hell. The choice is ours, but just like the surfer, we need to practice- to learn the art. The surfer's paradise is an alchemy between himself and the wave, thus he must include both the nature of the wave and that of his body in his "self awareness." Humanities' paradise is an alchemy between itself and the earth, thus it must include both the nature of the earth and that of its collective "body" in its "self awareness." Our "self awareness" must encompass the whole planet. This would automatically bring about a unity among humans, as it is our detachment from the earth that allows a detachment from each other. In one body of one mind, the right hand does not war with the left.

This "body" of humanity that we all are a part of might learn the "art" from other "bodies" on the earth that are already involved in an alchemy between themselves and the earth. These are the bodies of water that, like humanity, have both an individual form (as in water drops- rain) and a collective form (as in lakes and seas). Water has a tremendous effect on this planet. The earth is "more" as a result of interaction with water. Can humanity say this about its interaction with the earth? Water embraces the earth and nurtures it, thus creating a potential neither would have alone. Water and earth surrender to each other at a plane of mutual existence. This results in an alchemy from which blossoms a condition we call life. All aspects of this condition we call life have continued the alchemical interaction, the embracing, the nurturing, with each other and the earth. These characteristics, originating from water, have been inherent in all life forms instinctively and naturally until humanity. *Humanity has broken the tradition of embracing and nurturing the earth.* We must re-learn from the waters, how to relate to our earth. Humanity must relate to the earth as water does. We must embrace, nurture, surrender, encounter, interact, and transform ourselves and the earth in a plane of mutual existence. This is a way to realize our potential. *We will only enter the heavens through the earth.*

Tree, you are a sign of life
        with fruit and fowl and shade
You are a pleasure just to see
        as you tousle in the breeze

It takes so long for you to grow
        to be what you are now
Yet I must cut you down
        to do my part in destroying all
        that is beautiful.

Conceptual Awareness

If we conceptualize our relationship to the planet, we find:

We are like a lizard eating itself by starting with the tail; eventually the damage starts to outweigh the nourishment.

If we look at this and accept it, we have made the first step toward survival as a species. This is a conceptual awareness of our status. We are good at finding solutions. Our weakness seems to be in recognizing the problem.

Conscious Application

After we become aware of something as serious as damage to "ourselves", we suddenly find ourselves "inspired" to apply our powers to save ourselves. Thus *conceptual awareness* sparks *conscious application*. We apply ourselves to the limits of the somewhat meager stage of consciousness we have allowed ourselves. This conscious application can take place both collectively through social arenas and individually through alliance with natural phenomenon. Since social entities are made up of individuals, they should ultimately follow the course of the *majority* of the individuals. However, individuals, having lost their alliance with natural phenomenon for the most part, have no course. Consequently, the present social entities (political and corporate) have evolved such a collective and powerful "ego" that they herd and lead individuals like sheep. They subtly and daily tell individuals what and who they are and what they need. Then they, the political and corporate entities, provide it in a way that manifests great stress both to the individuals and the planet.

This situation can be reversed simply by choice - a choice as simple as a surfer deciding to learn to ride a wave rather than being tossed around and abused by it. Individuals can take steps aligned with natural phenomenon, make moves, and consciously and independently apply themselves toward a *direct means of survival*. This means by-passing what has turned out to be the "middle man" between individuals and survival, i.e. those political and corporate entities. If enough individuals do this, the massive political and corporate dinosaurs that *herd* individuals will become "beasts" that *serve* individuals. Our individual steps are arrows that penetrate dogma. Penetration of dogma by the majority will result in *less powerful* agencies of social convenience as opposed to the current *more powerful* agencies of social oppression. With less government and corporate "care", individuals can directly take charge and care of themselves via *direct communion with the planet.* If we do not take ourselves there, the powers that "be" will take us. Direct communion with the planet will lead us to a plane of mutual existence where we will find peace and unity.

Individual conscious application toward direct communication with the planet can make survival "a song sung while living." This means *daily,* moment to moment, applying ones self toward *direct means of living.* Mutual exchange with the earth is not stressful on either the earth or the individual. This is the nature of a plane of mutual existence. There is much power here. There is also paradise.

Direct living is by-passing, as often as possible and in any way possible, all of the centralized political and corporate dinosaurs that currently herd us like sheep and provide us with "food", energy and shelter, and a way of life. They are, in effect, steering our very evolution. To actually stop these political and corporate dinosaurs from devastating the earth in order to "take care of us" is virtually impossible. They have now their own collective wills and egos to nourish by telling us what we need, then raping the earth to provide us with it for a price that has to sustain their phenomenal rate of inefficiency and level of greed. However, if we suddenly decide what we need ourselves and then proceed to directly trade with and encounter the earth to acquire it; we won't need political and corporate dinosaurs. It is our need that feeds them. Without our need, their power will diminish and we as individuals will find ourselves experiencing direct living.

Direct living is finding a plane of mutual existence between our housing and the earth. This means orienting the design of housing and the concept of living itself toward the prevailing natural phenomenon rather than the prevailing "marketable design." This, in turn, means housing that is heated and/or cooled and energized directly by the existing natural energies of the area. The architects must put forth designs that "ride" these energies in such a way that the home, by its very nature, takes care of the owner. This must happen without stress to either the owner or the planet. This will reduce the need for the "care" that the political and corporate dinosaurs provide at extreme stress to both people and planet.

These "dinosaurs" provide "care" via centralized energy systems that produce and distribute energy by collecting and burning fossil and atomic fuels. These systems are rapidly lowering our quality of life through destruction of our host of life- the earth. In addition, centralized energy systems require a lacing of the earth with an ever-growing spider web of dangerous cables which themselves further lower the quality of life by disturbing natural processes and natural beauty. These power lines breed human dependance on that lower quality of life. If you don't want a 350kv power line in your back yard, then you should take steps now to get off of the power grid. The long range distribution of electricity is subject to line resistance which results in the production of twice as much energy as there is actually a demand for. This kind of inefficiency alone should be enough reason to dispense with centralized production of energy.

The production of our food has also become centralized. Farmlands are being bought up by large corporate chains that "make" food grow with chemicals. Direct living means growing, and finding, as much of our own food as possible. This, of course, means evolving our diet. Food from the corporate dinosaurs consumes vast amounts of energy and vitality from the earth both in "money oriented" production and in long-range distribution. *Money oriented production of food also radically effects the quality of the food to the extent that the food itself becomes a detriment to ones health.* De-centralized production of food, both individually and communally, results in better food and a positive exchange with the planet. The current methods of centralized food production and distribution do not result in an exchange with the planet. They simply take from the planet while removing us from natural processes which themselves are "patterns" that can guide our conscious evolution.

Centralized production of energy and food radically increases the power of money as money becomes the *only* avenue through which we can obtain our sustenance. The monetary system has become an entity (almost a god) in itself through which we attain our existence from the political corporate dinosaurs. The more we obtain directly from the earth through positive exchange, the less we have to buy. Direct living means reducing the power of money and increasing the power of direct interaction with the earth, the sun, other individuals, etc. to fulfill our needs. A fundamental aspect of direct living is reducing and scrutinizing our needs themselves- "living simply so others may simply live."

Direct living also means recognizing the by-products of our civilization as "natural resources" of our age and using them accordingly. This means recycling- *using* our garbage rather than burying it or tossing it out the window. Even our garbage is energy that can be ridden.

Physical Manifestation

Conscious application (i.e. a direct living state of mind) paves the way for physical manifestation. The photo shows a physical manifestation of direct living. This home makes its own electricity from the sun. It also makes domestic hot water from the sun. Its interior walls are constructed from recycled aluminum cans and glass bottles. Its foundations are composed of recycled automobile tires. It has a food producing greenhouse. The water from the lavatory, kitchen sink and bath tubs are reused as grey water in planters that grow food.

The most security I can imagine
is being able to shift my
point of view.

The Shift

Direct living involves a slight shift in consciousness-viewing things from a different vantage point. This slight shift is the beginning step toward the maneuverability discussed in the previous chapter. If we become adept at these slight shifts, soon we will find ourselves maneuvering through our problems rather than becoming them.

When a baby is learning to walk, it takes a lot of short steps at first. Then, gradually, longer steps are taken. Soon it is walking from point to point. Learning to maneuver is similar, only the steps are "shifts." An example of one such shift follows.

Look at an aluminum beverage can. For years this item has been distributed all over the globe as a container for beverages consumed by human beings. The beverage can is so well distributed over the planet that it is at least as common and plentiful as wood. It has been looked upon as waste or garbage- therefore worthless. For a long time beverage cans were thrown anywhere and everywhere. Then they became a problem to the environment. Reluctantly and solely as a result of pressure from various environmental movements, the manufacturers of beverage cans began to recycle the aluminum to make more beverage cans.

Now, we have something that is as plentiful as wood 2x4's and actually available in more places that 2x4's. Shelters and homes around the world have been built of whatever can be found in the area; from grass reeds, to trees, to rocks, to mud, etc. All of these things appear naturally on the planet. Beverage cans appear "naturally" on the planet and are found in more places than any of the above mentioned "standard" building materials. *The shift is now.* We must shift our way of looking at a beverage can. They will last as long and function very similar to a concrete block or a brick. In fact, they are "natural" bricks. The shift is in looking at beverage cans from a different point of view- the other side of the orbit (see chapter four)- releasing the garbage stigma. Many of these types of shifts are necessary to begin to maneuver, and maneuver we must if we are to evolve fast enough to change before we destroy our host organism - the earth.

In Taos, New Mexico, beverage cans have been used for building since 1972. The techniques have evolved over the years to the point where they are approved by state building codes (on an individual basis) and financial institutions. The beverage can is a low tech, energy efficient building product, the collection and use of which creates minimum skilled employment; cleans up the environment; provides shelter; and reduces the demand for more precious natural resources (like trees) all in one "shift." This is only a single shift. Imagine what can be accomplished in groups of shifts and eventually

through the ability to actually "maneuver." *Small shifts in our point of view will show us more appropriate ways to deal with our present way of life ... Maneuvering will show us a different way of life.*

There are many physical manifestations of direct living that follow in this chapter. They represent a "shifting" and "moving" from the traditional architectural concepts of human habitats. They represent the beginning of a journey to a less stressful (to both human and planet) and more appropriate way of life.

ONE LOW-TECH SKILL AND TWO MATERIALS (ONE OF WHICH IS A BY-PRODUCT OF OUR SOCIETY) MAKE BOTH WALLS AND ROOF OF A LOW MAINTAINENCE STRUCTURE THAT WILL LAST MANY LIFETIMES. INSULATION IS PLACED IN THE SPACE BETWEEN THE WALLS AS THEY GO UP.

THE COMBINATION OF HUMAN BY-PRODUCTS, HUMAN ENERGY AND SIMPLE CARING IS AN ALCHEMY THAT CAN PRODUCE A HUMAN SHELTER. THIS IS SHELTER PRODUCED WITH MINIMAL USE OF FOSSEL FUEL ENERGY, CORPORATE PRODUCTS AND HIGH TECHNOLOGY. THIS IS AN APPLICATION OF THE CONCEPT OF DIRECT LIVING.

Caring is
the seed of
a new Reality.

THIS PHOTO WAS TAKEN FROM INSIDE THE DOME SHOWN ON THE PREVIOUS PAGE. THE WINDOWS ARE 55 GALLON OIL DRUMS CUT IN HALF. OPPOSITE IS A VAULTED HALLWAY ALSO MADE OF ALUMINUM CANS LAID IN CEMENT. THESE SHAPES AND SPACES ILLUSTRATE THE VERSITILITY OF THE ALUMINUM CAN "BRICK." DUE TO THE FACT THAT ALUMINUM CANS ARE SO LIGHT, THESE SHAPES CAN BE CONSTRUCTED WITHOUT THE FORMWORK NECESSARY IN CLAY BRICK MASONRY. HOMES, COMMUNITIES, EVEN CITIES COULD BE BUILT WITH THIS MATERIAL AS THEY HAVE BEEN BUILT IN THE PAST WITH TRADITIONAL CLAY BRICKS.

THIS IS NOT TO SAY THE USE OF ALUMINUM CANS FOR BUILDING IS GOING TO SOLVE THE PROBLEMS OF OUR WORLD. HOWEVER, THE TYPE OF THINKING THAT ALLOWS THE ALUMINUM CAN TO "BE" A BRICK IS A STEP IN THE RIGHT DIRECTION. THIS TYPE OF THINKING LENDS US THE FLEXIBILITY TO UNINHIBITEDLY RESPOND TO THE NATURE OF THE MOMENT ... AND AT THE MOMENT WE HAVE MORE OF WHAT WE TERM "GARBAGE" THAN ANY OTHER NATURAL RESOURCE.

TREES DROP THEIR LEAVES TO THE
GROUND. THE LEAVES ROT AT THE
BASE OF THE TREE, THUS ENRICH-
ING THE SOIL FROM WHICH THE
TREE GETS ITS NOURISHMENT. THE
TREE (BY STRATEGIC PLACEMENT
OF ITS BY-PRODUCT- LEAVES) IS
CONSTANTLY CONTRIBUTING TO
ITS EXISTENCE. LIKEWISE, WE AS
HUMANS (BY STRATEGIC PLACE-
MENT AND USE OF OUR OWN BY-
PRODUCTS) CAN CONSTANTLY BE
CONTRIBUTING TO, RATHER THAN
TAKING FROM OUR EXISTENCE.

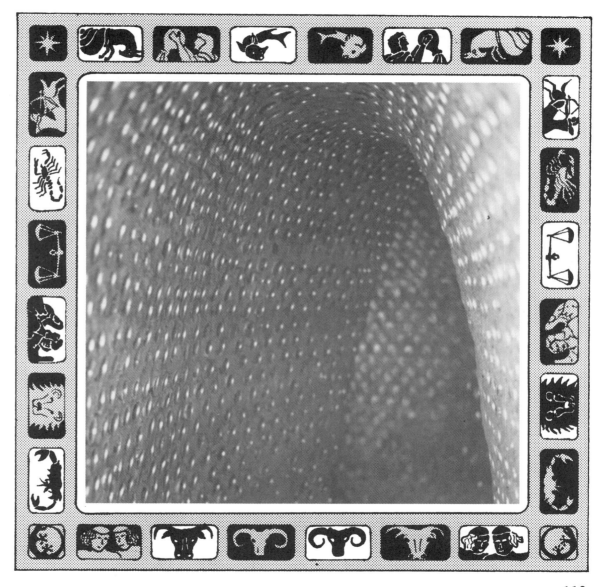

THIS PHOTO IS A CONSTRUCTION SHOT OF THE BUILDING ILLUSTRATED IN THE DRAWINGS OPPOSITE. THE FOLLOWING FOUR PAGES ARE ALSO PHOTOS OF THAT BUILDING. THESE THREE DOMES MADE OF ALUMINUM CANS WERE TOTALLY BURIED WHICH REVEALS THE STRENGTH OF THIS METHOD OF CONSTRUCTION.

LIVING

skylite

KITCHEN

BATH

FLOOR PLAN

112

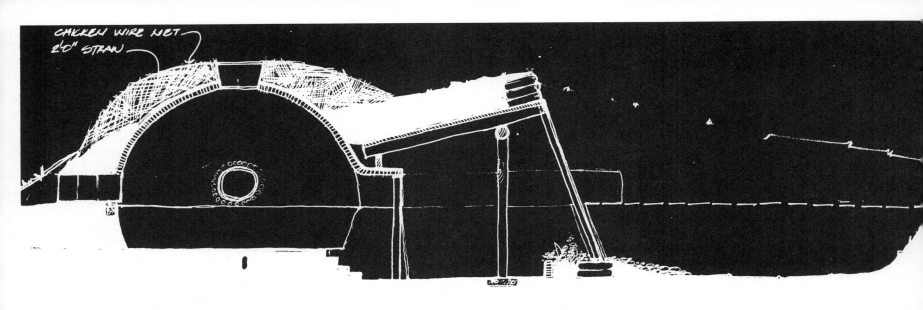

CHICKEN WIRE NET
2'0" STRAN

SECTION AT DOME
SECTION BETWEEN DOMES

LINE OF
EXISTING GRADE

113

VAULTED HALLWAYS THAT TURN
INTO DOMES, ILLUSTRATE THE UN-
LIMITED POSSIBILITIES OF THIS
NATURAL "BRICK."

THE DOMES WERE PLASTERED AND THEN BURIED, THUS REDUCING THE NEED FOR INSULATION AND ROOFING.

THE BURIED DOMES OPENED UP THE EXCITING POSSIBILITY OF UNDERGROUND LABRINTHS, ALL MADE WITH TWO MATERIALS AND ONE LOW-TECH SKILL. THUS THE TERM "BURYING OUR GARBAGE" HAS A "SHIFTED" MEANING.

ALUMINUM CAN DOMES HAD TO BE PRESENTED TO THE PUBLIC, i.e. THE REAL ESTATE MARKET, IN SMALL DOSES AS APPENDAGES OF MORE TRADITIONAL STRUCTURES. THIS SOUTHWESTERN STYLED SOLAR ADOBE HOME SERVED WELL AS A "SAFE ACT" WITHIN WHICH TWO ALUMINUM CAN DOMES WERE INTRODUCED. THIS PROJECT MARKED THE SUCCESFUL ENTRY OF ALUMINUM CAN DOMES INTO THE REAL WORLD.

THIS IS A PICTURE OF A MAN EXPERIENCING THE PLANE OF MUTUAL EXISTENCE WITH A CHICKEN NAMED MARTHA. THE WALL OF MARTHA'S CHICKEN COUP IS SEEN IN THE BACKGROUND. IT IS A HALF DOME (OPEN ON SOUTH SIDE) MADE OF BOTTLES AND ALUMINUM CANS SET ON A FOUNDATION OF AUTOMOBILE TIRES TIGHTLY PACKED WITH EARTH.

WHILE THE HALF DOMES (OPPOSITE PAGE) AND FULL DOMES (PREVIOUS PAGES) REPRESENT THE PUREST FORM OF USING RECYCLED CANS AND BOTTLES FOR CONSTRUCTION, THEY ARE NOT THE ONLY WAY.

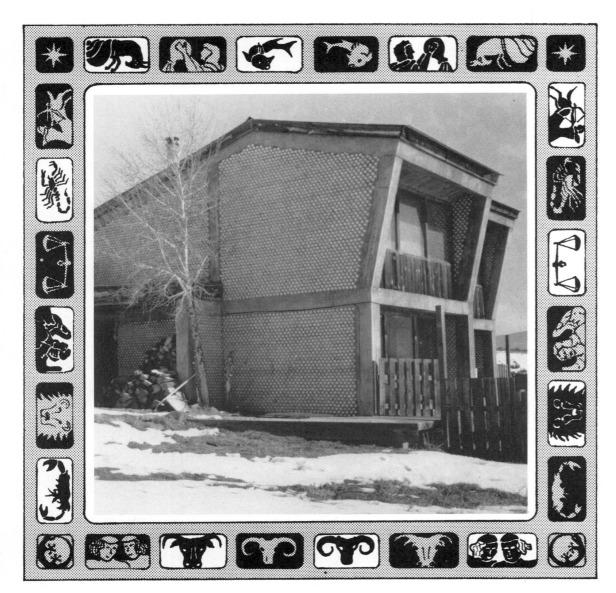

THIS BUILDING WAS BUILT USING ALUMINUM CANS IN A PANEL WALL. THE PANELS ARE (LIKE THE DOMES) A DOUBLE THICKNESS OF CANS LAID IN CEMENT WITH INSULATION IN THE MIDDLE. THIS CREATES A SANDWICH PANEL ABOUT 14 INCHES THICK. THIS METHOD ALLOWS FOR MORE CONVENTIONAL SHAPES AND DETAILS.

THE POST AND BEAM STRUCTURE
IS CONVENTIONAL AND COULD BE
WOOD, CONCRETE OR STEEL. NO
FINISH IS REQUIRED INSIDE OR
OUT. THE RESULT IS AN INEX-
PENSIVE PANEL THAT ULTIMATE-
LY REQUIRES NO MAINTANIENCE.

IF DESIRED, A TOTALLY SOUTH-WESTERN APPEARANCE CAN BE ACHIEVED. MANY SOUTHWESTERN STYLED HOMES HAVE BEEN BUILT WITH ALUMINUM CANS. THE CANS HAVE PROVED TO BE AS "FLUID" AS ADOBE FOR DESIGN AND DETAILING, YET MUCH MORE DURABLE. CANS AND BOTTLES ARE BECOMING VALUABLE BUILDING MATERIALS IN NEW MEXICO.

IN NATURE THERE IS NO SUCH THING AS GARBAGE. GARBAGE IS SIMPLY A CONCEPT OF THE HUMAN DOGMA.

A PYRAMID ON THE MESA NEAR TAOS WAS ALSO BUILT OF ALUMINUM CANS LAID IN A CEMENT MORTAR. THIS CONSTRUCTION PHOTO ILLUSTRATES THE STRUCTURE OF THE ALUMINUM CAN DOME WITHIN THE FOUR LEANING ALUMINUM CAN WALLS OF THE PYRAMID. SAND FILLS THE SPACE BETWEEN THE DOME AND THE LEANING WALLS. BECAUSE THE ALUMINUM CAN WALLS ARE SO LIGHTWEIGHT, THE SAND FILL ACTUALLY SUPPORTS THEM AS THEY IN TURN CONTAIN THE SAND.

THERE IS NO MATERIAL, OTHER
THAN ALUMINUM CANS, THAT
COULD HAVE FACILITATED THIS
PARTICULAR STRUCTURAL DESIGN
CONCEPT.

If we don't know what to do
with the by-product. . .
We shouldn't use the
product.

125

ONCE THE "SHIFT" HAD BEEN MADE, OTHER BY-PRODUCTS OF OUR MATERIAL WORLD BEGAN TO CHANGE FROM GARBAGE TO NATURAL RESOURSES. USED AUTOMOBILE TIRES TIGHTLY PACKED WITH EARTH CREATE A TWO AND ONE HALF FOOT THICK THERMAL MASS WALL THAT IS ALSO LOAD BEARING. OPPOSITE IS THE FIRST EXPERIMENTAL STRUCTURE USING THIS TECHNIQUE IN COMBINATION WITH ALUMINUM CANS. HERE, THE TECHNIQUE HAS BEEN REFINED TO AN ART.

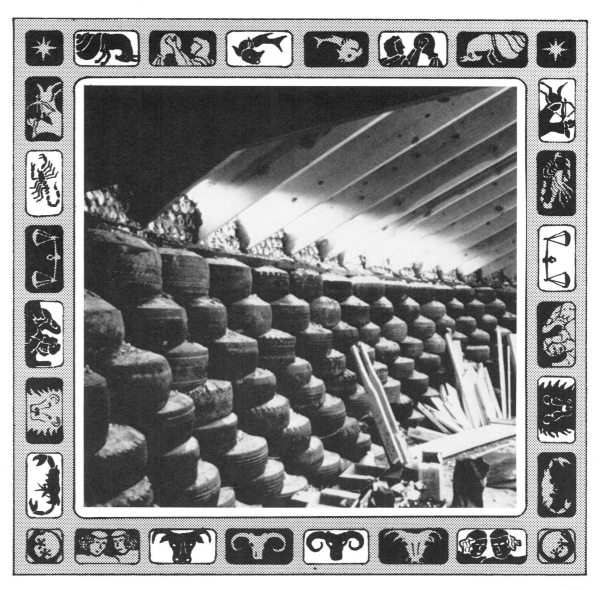

In addition to allowing garbage to appear as a natural resource, the "shift" is what has allowed solar energy for heating and energizing homes to become a part of our reality. Of course, the various energy scares we have had (from the "oil shortage" to the Russian power plant catastrophe) have "inspired" this shift.

The use of solar energy is one of the few examples in our modern civilization of riding universal energy patterns. Solar energy is a universal energy, the patterns of which we are slowly learning to recognize as we begin to accept, align, and transform it, i.e., as we learn to "ride" it.

There was once, and still is, a small company called World Energy and Materials in Taos, New Mexico, that built solar, energy efficient homes out of garbage. In the process of developing solar housing in the late seventies, they "rode" a major energy "wave" of the swarm of humanity- the U.S. government. This is a perfect example of riding energy (that of human nature) to develop housing that rides energy, that of the sun. The result was a government-financed step toward direct living for many people. This is a real application of the "outlaw" example of riding energy discussed in the previous chapter.

The small company accepted and aligned with the existing energy patterns of FmHA. That is, they accepted FmHA as a substantial source of funds for producing housing while recognizing the housing left much to be desired from any standpoint, not to mention the concept of direct living.

Alignment with FmHA allowed the small company to begin building FmHA housing and established a rapport with FmHA. Thus, the small company allowed themselves to *encounter* FmHA.

Further, the small company, which was made up of working people who themselves needed housing and jobs, began to slowly and subtly *transform* certain aspects of the rigid FmHA program toward the concepts of direct living- specifically toward solar underground housing. This was made possible because they allowed themselves to *encounter* FmHA rather than *resist* it. The transformation came about very slowly. First, some south facing windows; next, some strategic roof angles; next, slightly submerged floor levels; until finally, FmHA was financing solar underground housing.

At this point, many of the workers of the small company, applied for FmHA loans and got them because they had steady jobs building FmHA housing for the small company.

So the workers became the clients and the FmHA money was used to develop solar underground housing for the small company's workers while also providing them with employment. The loan monies, (as much as $250,000 in one year) were granted to a specific worker who then paid the small company, his employer, for a solar underground house. Then the small company paid that very worker, and his fellow workers, a salary to build his house. The FmHA money was used like a ping pong ball, back and forth to provide jobs, homes, and to pursue direct living concepts all for the same people. It was like a grant. Everyone was being paid to research and develop direct living concepts while getting a home at the same time. No one agreed with the FmHA program to start with. It was much like an offensive wind. However, *encounter* and *transformation* turned this program into a research and development grant providing jobs and homes for a new age much like a windmill takes an offensive wind and makes it pump life-giving water.

This photo is the result- a small community of solar oriented underground homes. This is direct living financed by the U.S. government. This is an example of riding energy to achieve further energy riding. These are very simple but very tangible steps toward direct living.

The solar underground house developed for this project was called the "Volkshome" (people's home) after the volkswagon car which was the forerunner of the energy efficient "people's cars", i.e. cars that the majority of people could afford to purchase and operate.

The following is a section of the volkshome and a floor plan.

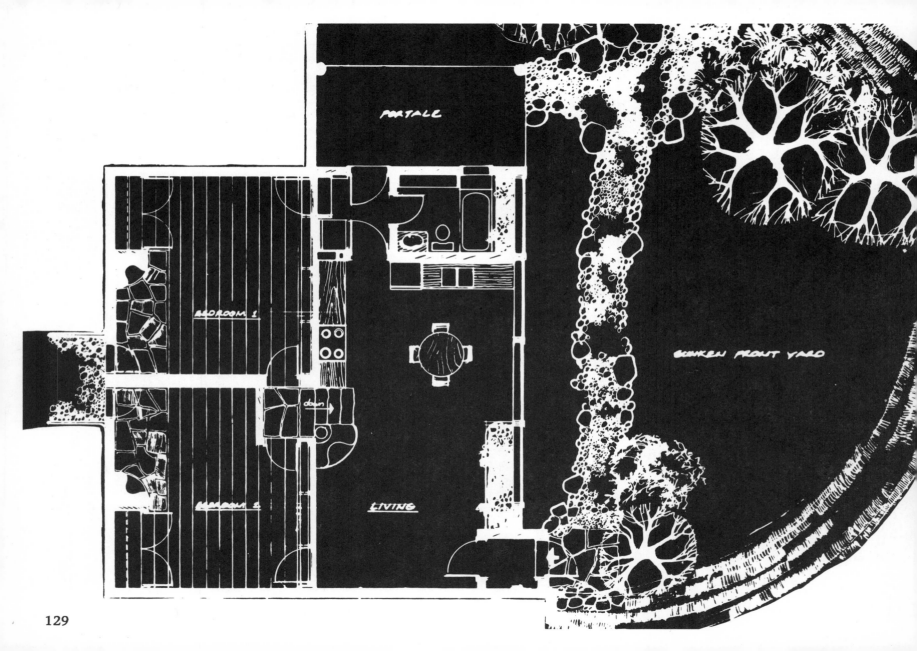

PORTALE

BEDROOM 1

down

BEDROOM 2

LIVING

SUNKEN FRONT YARD

129

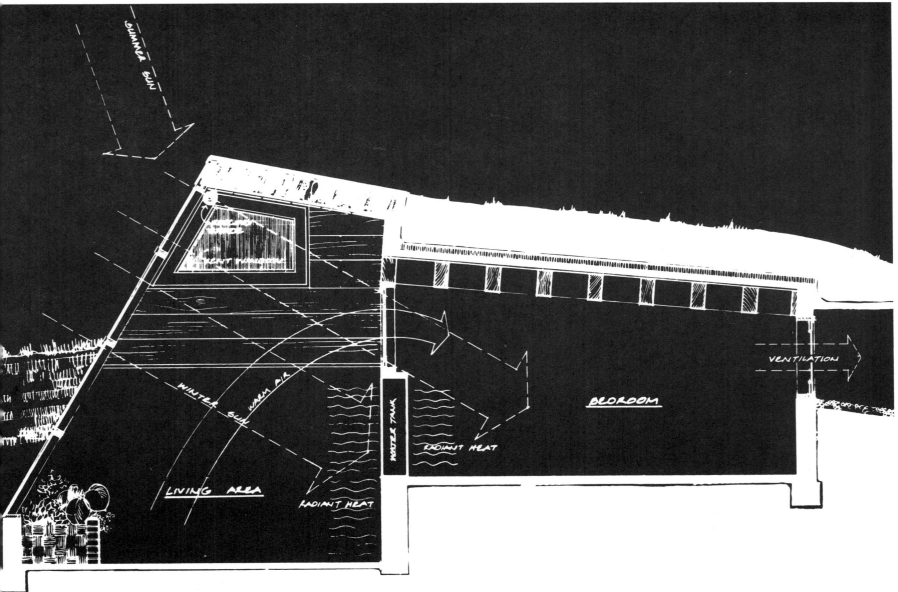

SUMMER SUN

WINTER SUN

WARM AIR

WATER TANK

RADIANT HEAT

LIVING AREA

RADIANT HEAT

BEDROOM

VENTILATION

THE VOLKSHOME DEVELOPMENTAL PROCESS TOOK PLACE OVER ABOUT A TEN YEAR PERIOD. WHILE PROVIDING HOMES AND JOBS, THE FmHA MONIES WERE BASICALLY USED FOR RESEARCH AND DEVELOPMENT OF SOLAR UNDERGROUND HOUSING. THIS KNOWLEDGE WAS THEN PUT TOGETHER WITH THE REFINED ALUMINUM CAN AND TIRE CONSTRUCTION TECHNIQUES AND A HOME WAS DEVELOPED EMPLOYING THE BEST OF ALL THAT WAS LEARNED. THE RESULT (SEE PHOTO AND DRAWINGS OPPOSITE) IS A HOME MADE OF BASICALLY FREE RECYCLED MATERIALS THAT WOULD OTHERWISE HAVE BEEN TERMED "GARBAGE". THIS HOME MAKES ITS OWN HEAT, ELECTRICITY, AND HOT WATER FROM ENCOUNTERS WITH THE SUN. IT GROWS FOOD INSIDE AND REUSES ITS GREY WATER. THIS IS A 95% SELF-SUFFICIENT HOME THAT ENCOUNTERS THE EARTH, THE SUN, AND THE BY-PRODUCTS OF HUMANITY ITSELF. THIS IS A HOME AND A WAY OF LIFE THAT TRULY RIDES THE ENERGY PATTERNS AT HAND.

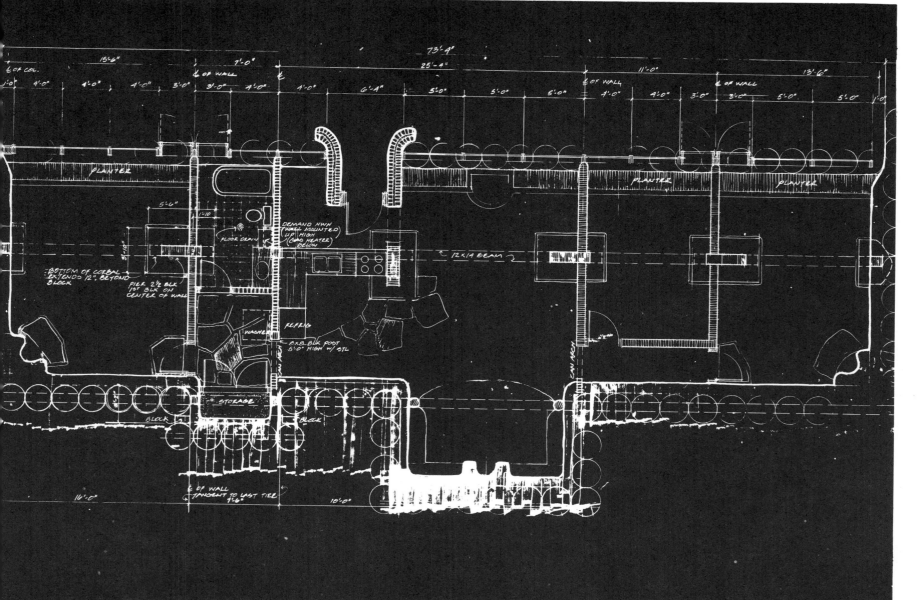

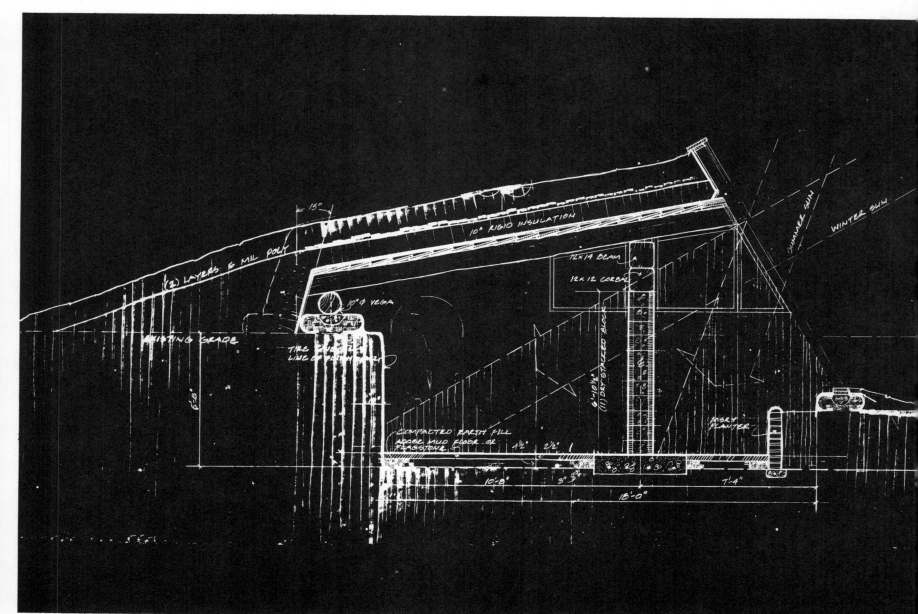

EVERY PROJECT LEANS FURTHER IN THE DIRECTION OF MAKING HOUSING AVAILABLE TO PEOPLE WITH LESS STRESS TO THEM AND TO THE PLANET. THE DETAILS GET MORE SIMPLE WHILE THE PERFORMANCE GETS BETTER. WE ARE LEARNING TO RIDE THE WAVES BOTH OF THE EARTH AND OF OURSELVES.

WE ARE DEVELOPING AN "EARTH SHIP." THIS PROJECT IS A PROTOTYPE FOR A DESIGN TO BE USED AND BUILT BY THE HOMELESS. A WHOLE NEW BY-PRODUCT OF OUR SOCIETY, THE HOMELESS ARE A PHENOMENON OF THE HOLLOW ECONOMY OF THE UNITED STATES IN THE LATE 80'S AND EARLY 90'S. DIRECT LIVING CAN REDUCE THE DEPENDANCE ON THIS HOLLOW ECONOMY AND LEAD THE HOMELESS TO A WAY OF LIFE THAT EVEN THE WEALTHY WILL SOON BE STRUGGLING FOR.

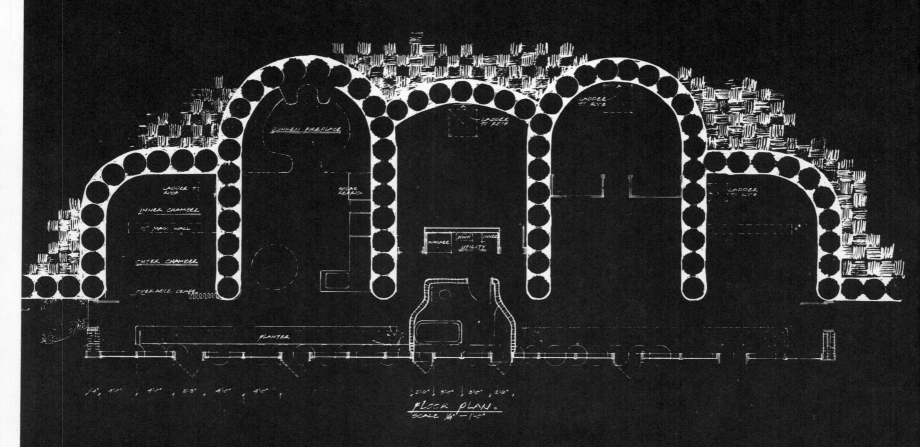

SUNKEN FIREPLACE

LADDER TO ROOF

LADDER TO ROOF

SOLAR HEATING

LADDER TO ROOF

INNER CHAMBER

10" MAS. WALL

OUTER CHAMBER

OVERHEAD DRAPE

WASHER | HWH | DRYER
UTILITY

PLANTER

FLOOR PLAN.
SCALE 1/8" = 1'-0"

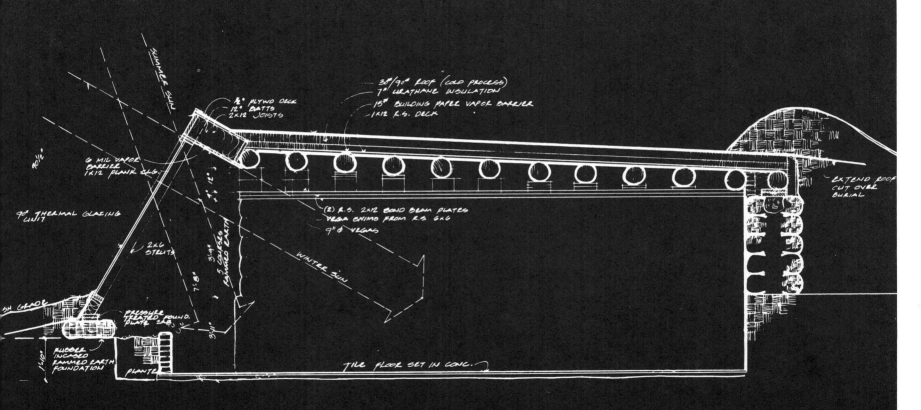

SUMMER SUN

3# /90° ROOF (COLD PROCESS)
7" URATHANE INSULATION
15# BUILDING PAPER VAPOR BARRIER
1X12 R.S. DECK

½" PLYWD DECK
12" BATTS
2X12 JOISTS

6 MIL VAPOR
BARRIER
1X12 PLANK CLG.

90° THERMAL GLAZING
UNIT

90½°

(2) R.S. 2X12 BOND BEAM PLATES
VEGA SHIMO FROM R.S. 6X6
9" Ø VEGAS

2X6
STRUTS

EXTEND ROOF
CUT OVER
BURIAL

7'-8"   7'-3½"

3'4"
5 COURSES
RAMMED EARTH

WINTER SUN

EX GRADE

PRESSURE
TREATED FOUND.
PLATE 2X6

3'4"

RUBBER
INCASED
RAMMED EARTH
FOUNDATION

1'-10"

PLANTER

TILE FLOOR SET IN CONC.

STRUCTURAL SECTION
SCALE ½"=1'-0"

THIS IS DIRECT LIVING- NEW AND
FORGOTTEN APPROACHES TO OUR
EXISTING WAY OF LIFE. THIS WILL
BUY US TIME TO EVOLVE OTHER
WAYS OF LIFE AS WE MOVE TO-
WARD OUR POTENTIAL- WHICH IS
THE IMAGE OF GOD.

The small company continues to pursue even more "low tech" applications of direct living. The following drawings were financed by the National Endowment for the Arts. They illustrate a building that encounters the earth, the sun, the wind and human garbage.

This building is a basic solar underground configuration setting on an earth-rammed tire wall. The shape of the building and landscaping is coned up to orient wind into the vertical axis windmill on top. The windmill produces electricity for the house.

The windmill is called a "dynasphere" and is a low tech design that can be manufactured in any small town that has a welder. This home grows food inside, reuses its grey water, gets heat and hot water from the sun, stores heat in the earth, and gets electricity from the wind. It is a refined version of the first building pictured in this chapter.

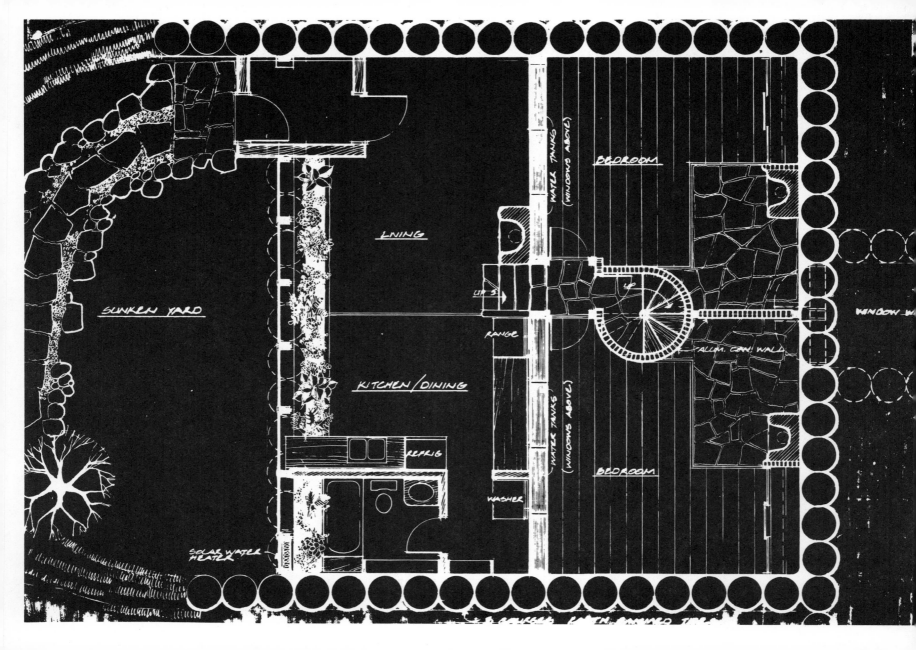

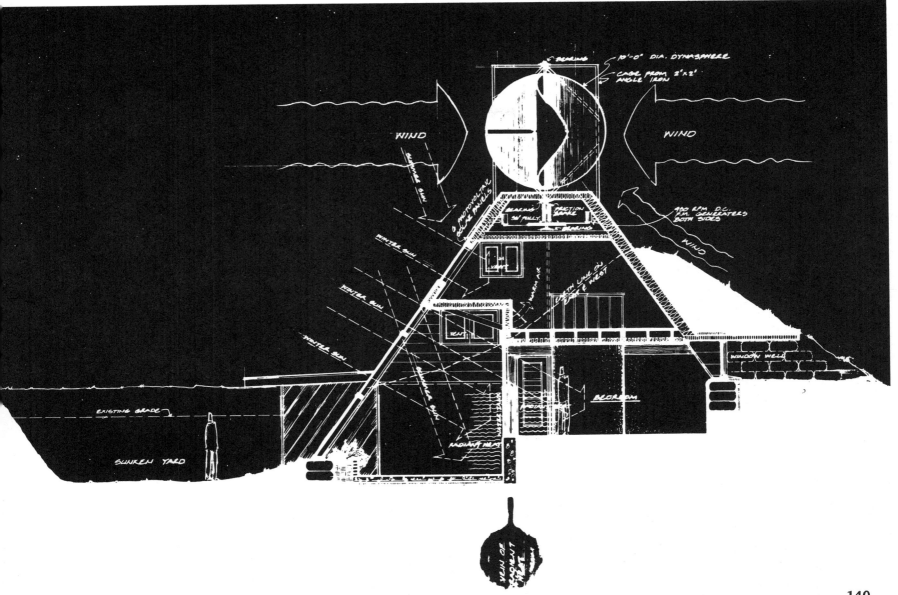

WIND

WIND

WIND

10'-0" DIA. DYNASPHERE

CAGE FROM 2"x2"
ANGLE IRON

BEARING

480 R.P.M. D.C.
F.M. GENERATORS
BOTH SIDES

PHOTOVOLTAIC SOLAR PANELS

SUMMER SUN

FRICTION DRIVE

BEARING
5" PULLY
5" BEARING

WINTER SUN

WINTER SUN

WARM AIR

EARTH LINE ON E WEST

WINTER SUN

VENT

WINDOW WELL

BEDROOM

RADIANT

EXISTING GRADE

RADIANT HEAT

SUNKEN YARD

140

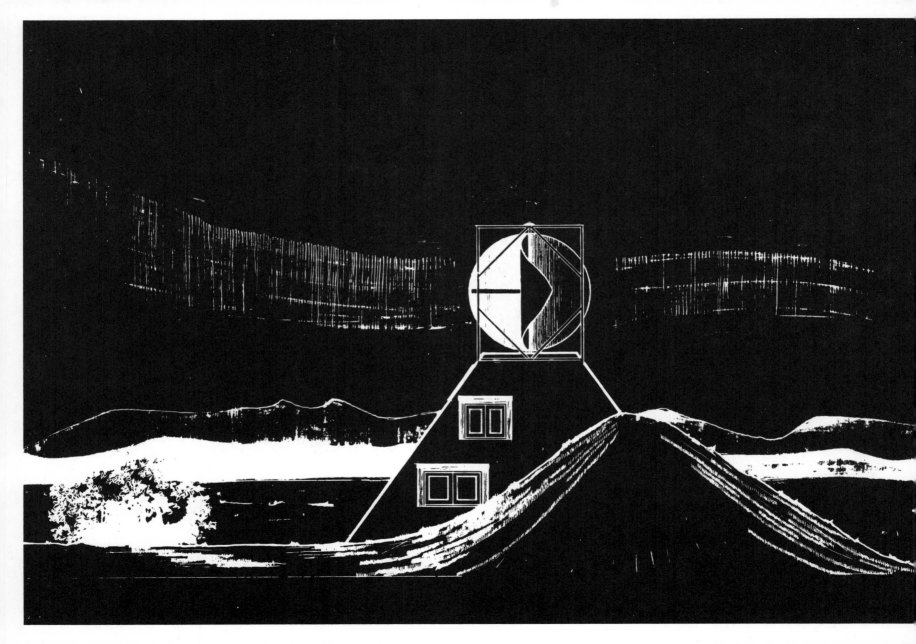

Beyond Direct Living

The buildings in this chapter illustrate many aspects of the concept of direct living as it relates to architecture. While these examples are a vivid application of direct living, they are by no means the *only* application. The direct living attitude can be applied to agriculture, medicine, economics, education, and even politics. Direct living is a state of mind out of which a reality is manifesting.

Direct living makes use of the existing roots of our existing reality. It involves new and forgotten approaches to an *existing* overall concept of life. Direct living will buy us the time and mind space to allow and participate in our own evolution. Our own evolution will in turn take us beyond our present concept of life.

Direct living is an immediate, tangible step we can take now. It will move us into closer contact with the unarguable phenomenon that we will eventually "ride" beyond direct living and beyond our existing concept of life.

Imagine if someone offered you
        a choice between two automobiles.
Both look basically the same.
Both cost about the same.
Both handle much the same.
However, one consumes gasoline
        and the other consumes nothing.

Which one would you choose?

CHAPTER SIX
THE ART OF LEANING

The Way

From the top of a mountain ridge, one can get a more all-encompassing view of the approach to life in the lower lands below. The unique enlightenment gained from this type of view is unattainable without somehow getting oneself up to the ridge line of the mountains to experience it. If one decides or discovers or believes this view is worthwhile, then one must find a pathway up to the top of the mountain. There is a vision on the top of the mountain. To intellectualize about this vision is meaningless without actualizing a *way* of getting there to experience it. Likewise, an awareness of a more appropriate state of mind from which to view the universe is meaningless without an immediately tangible *way* to get to this state of mind.

The road to Nirvana is of no less significance than Nirvana itself.

Non-local awareness is the topic of the next chapter. The concept of non-local awareness is being submitted as a more appropriate method of relating to the universe. It is, however, a meaningless concept unless a way of getting to a state of mind suitable to experience it is illuminated. One such way of getting to a state of mind from which non-local awareness can be experienced is the *art of leaning*. Just as we must actualize a *way* to the top of the mountain before we can intellectualize a vision from there; we must, in this chapter, attempt to actualize a "way" to experience non-local awareness before we can intellectualize it. This "way" is the *art of leaning*.

Leaning is a method of "movement" practiced by all living things. It is a wave, or pattern, of the universe that we can "ride" to other realities. A very simple example of leaning is found in the banana plant in my office. My office is an underground room with south facing windows. The banana plant is against a back north wall. After being against this rear wall for several weeks, I noticed the plant leaning toward the light (the light being in a rather unnatural position relative to the plant). As time went on, it began to lean so much, I feared it would fall over and uproot itself. If I tried to bend the plant all at once, from its original position to its "leaned" position, it would have surely broken the stalk. Yet, it bent or leaned itself toward the light over a period of time. (See diagram opposite).

This banana plant illustrates that plants "lean" toward the light. They do this at their own pace over a period of time. They are flexible over time. Both flexibility and rigidity are functions of time. To bend the plant in one instant would have broken it. It was rigid relative to that instant of time. However, expanded time allowed it flexibility- to lean toward the light.

145

We, as human organisms, are the same as the banana plant in this respect. We can align ourselves with this particular phenomenon or pattern, and maneuver via it. We too are rigid relative to short spans of time, but we can lean and have leaned toward what we want over longer periods of time. Plants lean toward light without choice. We lean toward vision - **the vision of our choice. This 'choice' is our conscious participation in our own evolution.**

LIGHT

DELINEATION OF ROOM

VISION

DELINEATION OF DOGMA

In the case of the banana plant, the delineation of the room only allows light to enter through the south window. In the case of the human condition, the delineation of our dogma only allows vision, a form of light, to enter through "windows." Outside the room, light *is*. The plant would not have to lean. Outside our dogma, vision *is*. We would not have to lean. Leaning is the natural intention of organisms to reach out of whatever confines (rooms, realities, dogmas, etc.) toward light. Thus the art of leaning can be a pathway out of dogma toward vision- universal vision. Non-local awareness is a universal vision.

THE GROWTH OF DOGMA
Interdogmatic Vision vs.
Universal Vision

Plants simply lean toward the light. Humans now have a choice about which direction they lean towards. This wasn't always the case. *Unconscious* leaning is what took us out of the water and onto the land millions of years ago. Leaning took us up off "all fours" and into an upright position. Leaning took our brains from reptilian, to paleomammalian, to neomammalian. The neomammalian part of our brain represents its latest evolution. This part of the brain completely encompasses the other two parts and is commonly known as the thinking cap. Leaning was the "Force of the Wizard" behind evolution that has always helped us keep pace with the natural processes of the planet. Leaning is how we became what we are.

Somewhere along the line (possibly during the development of the neo-mammalian brain) we found consciousness and became aware of ourselves. It was at this point we invented dogma and began making our own choices. Dogma started as the foundation for ourselves (our egos) and as a *basis* for our own choices. (Fig. 1)

Then dogma began
to grow.

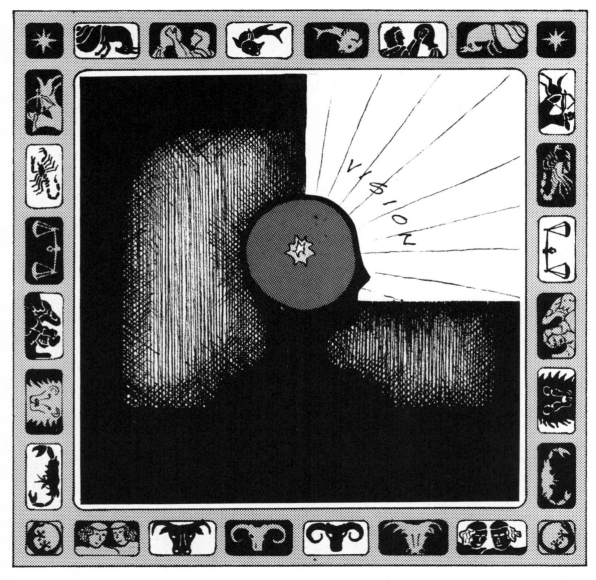

It grew into a protection
for our egos and
an influence on choice.

Now it has grown into a cocoon and it *dictates* choice. It has become a barrier between us and universal vision. The window through dogma is growing shut. The result of this is the introverted evolution which we are now experiencing. This is leaning toward visions that are simply images in and from our own dogma. They are not universal visions. They are not even broad enough to include the planet that we are an extension of. This is something like blocking off the windows in my office (previous diagram) and installing a grow light. The plant will lean toward the grow light no matter where it is placed. Likewise, in the absence of universal vision, *we* will lean toward "interdogmatic vision" no matter where it is "placed." Leaning is a "technique" of evolution. It can be directed by choice.

Before we attained consciousness and choice, nature made choices for us via what I have termed "The Wizard Energy." Nature, being without dogma, is an extension of universal vision. *So we were more intuitively in tune with the universe before and in the early stages of consciousness than we are now.* **Leaning was the method nature used to evolve us. Therefore it is appropriate that we use this same method to evolve ourselves.** Leaning is a method of movement, a "way." We can use this way to move ever closer to the patterns of the universe that sustain our existence, or we can use it to go around in circles until we "run out of gas."

We have let leaning take us from the foot path to the wheel. As our dogma began to close off the window to universal vision, *interdogmatic leaning* took us from the wheel to the automobile- a vision not broad enough to include the planet. Thus we have cities filled with carbon monoxide pollution and noise. We have yellow haze in the atmosphere belonging to this interdogmatic vision. We can continue to lean toward these narrow interdogmatic visions that do not include the planet, but we will eventually become extinct as a species because of the introverted evolution within our dogma. We can, however, stretch and lean out of dogma and toward universal vision if we choose to.

Universal vision is rooted in the patterns of the universe. It comes to us through galaxy, then solar system, then planet, then finally through our own dogma, if we are not so tightly closed that there is no window left. Universal vision includes our dogma but our dogma does not include universal vision. Leaning toward universal vision is blissful evolution toward light. The various unarguable phenomenon of our planet are our immediate directives for *universal vision.* Leaning toward *interdogmatic vision* will end up choking us one way or another just as the current "automobile vision" is doing.

Whatever one may think about the automobile-whether it is a vision that is not broad enough, or a useful tool, there is one unarguable fact; if you leave it running in your garage with the door closed to fresh air, it will kill you.

Whatever one may think about technology-whether it is a vision that is not broad enough, or a useful tool, presents one unarguable fact; if you "leave it running," on your earth with your vision closed to the earth's natural processes, it will kill you.

Technology, in general, is an interdogmatic vision that does not include the planet. Technology used with spherical vision would be a different story- so different it would probably not even be called technology. Technology only embraces the human ego in most cases. Thus, there are hundreds of polluted dump sites around the planet that are ruining water tables, land, atmosphere, etc. There are ever-increasing numbers of dams and power lines that ruin natural wild life patterns and ecosystems of the planet. There are ever-increasing numbers of various devices and machines that require raping the earth for fuel etc., etc., etc.

Interdogmatic visions do not know that we as humans are but an extension of the earth, so they do not consider it. Thus, they exploit it and dump on it. We are poisoning ourselves by our own hand because most of our vision does not include any more than our own back yards, much less the planet and beyond. It appears that, like the banana plant in my office, we could eventually lean so far in an "unnatural-natural" direction that we will simply fall away from the "pot" that sustains us and die as a species.

Universal vision would provide natural direction for leaning out toward vision beyond the limits of words. Words are a barrier that must be broken through. *When we invented words,a part of our dogma, we doomed ourselves to live within the limits of words.* Leaning is a method of movement that has no limitations. It is a way of consciously using flexibility and even fluidity through the media of time. If we use this "way" to go toward universal vision, we will find a more appropriate state of mind from which to relate to the universe.

155

This diagram shows the ever-tightening introverted evolution caused by our dogma (the human condition). Our vision is usually only as broad as the "self" area indicated on the ever-tightening spiral. Broader vision (i.e.expanded evolution) leads out of the spiral of dogma. Introverted evolution leads into the spiral of dogma to extinction. Self-oriented organisms move with no choice toward extinction. Many have before us. This is basically the same movement as that of matter to energy in the realm of physics. At the point of extinction, the matter has simply all moved back to energy- evolution to extinction. It is interesting to note that vision beyond words (i.e. light or energy- the entire area outside the spiral) exists both before the spiral of dogma and after it tightens to extinction. Before consciousness is found, organisms are simply victims of introverted evolution.They evolve toward extinction and, with no choice available, return to energy. However, now that we have found consciousness, we have a choice.

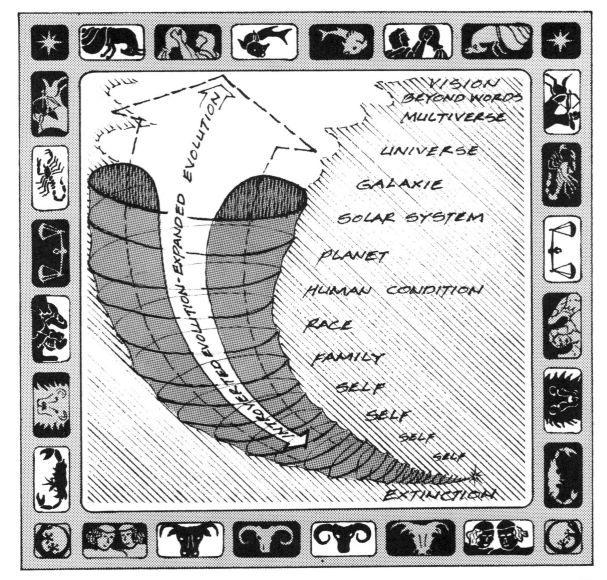

VISION
BEYOND WORDS
MULTIVERSE

UNIVERSE

GALAXIE

SOLAR SYSTEM

PLANET

HUMAN CONDITION

RACE

FAMILY

SELF

SELF

SELF

SELF

EXTINCTION

EVOLUTION - EXPANDED EVOLUTION

INTROVERTED EVOLUTION

We can reverse our introverted evolution and move toward expanded evolution and expand back to energy. Now, it is true, this is the same "place" we were going toward via introverted evolution anyway. The difference is that **via consciousness, we can choose the direction of our evolution and remain conscious through the process. We can consciously join the consciousness of the universe as opposed to unconsciously disintegrating into the consciousness of the universe. This is learning to "die" before we die, via consciousness.**

Introverted evolution is an unconscious leaning process toward extinction. Expanded evolution is the art of leaning, consciously used, to move toward energy (i.e. light, vision beyond words, etc.). A basic awareness of the leaning process will allow us to use it (to "ride" it as an unarguable phenomenon) for movement. Here is an example: when I became aware of the process of the plant leaning, I used it. Rather than prop up the plant, I rotated it so that it leaned against the wall. Now it is slowly growing back toward the light and becoming straight. If I keep rotating it periodically, I will be directing the growth of the plant by capitalizing on its own intention to lean toward light. If we as humans become aware of the various fundamental phenomenon of our existence (such as leaning) we can use this awareness to consciously direct our growth and thus freely maneuver both in and out of dogma. **There is nothing wrong with dogma if one can step in and out of it.**

Just as the flexibility of the banana plant was a function of time, our skill in the art of leaning (i.e. our ultimate flexibility) is a function of time. In the time span of one human life, we might observe that significant flexibility is somewhat limited. However, there is significant flexibility (movement-evolution) in the time span of all of the existence of humanity. Thus the art of leaning requires us to *view humanity as a whole* in one block of time via "spherical vision." We also must *change our concept of time* and make it work for us rather than against us.

157

God wants us to come home
by choice . . .
not just when our body
wears out.

Changing Our Concept of Time
One way to approach changing our concept of time is to change our current pattern of letting time tell us when to do things. In our current state of affairs, time hustles us through life with little "time" to spare. Time should be a friend, not a dictator. The friend will help us be flexible. The dictator will make us rigid.

We found natural increments of time through the movement of the earth around its own axis and around the sun. The movement of the moon around the earth further facilitated our "clocking" of natural increments of time. As our dogma grew, we began to manufacture clocks and watches, thus creating a rather "interdogmatic" version of time. The movement of the spheres through space guided us in relating to the natural patterns of the planet we were born on. The movement of our little minute and hour hands now tighten our "window" through dogma and actually separate us from those natural patterns of the spheres we were born out of. In our present reality, it appears that we are continuously trying to cram more into these shorter spans of interdogmatic time, thus we have invented the "rat race." We produce more products in less time; go further distances in less time; get the effect of swimming fifty laps in ten minutes with the new instant swimming exercise module. Now, if rigidity is a function of time (remember the plant appeared rigid over a short span of time but flexible over a longer span), then look at what we are doing with this rat race. We are making ourselves more rigid- that is, less capable of slowly leaning out of our dilemmas, because we do not allow anything to be done slowly anymore. If you only have ten minutes to do something, you don't have time to think about doing it any differently than you have always done it- thus you will become rigid. *Basically, time, like many other things (religion for one), has been found as a phenomenon and reproduced as a dogma and the result is rigidity.* Rigidity locks us in an unadaptable situation. If we reduce the emphasis on interdogmatic time (i.e. clocks, watches, scheduled living situations etc.) and increase the emphasis on natural time (i.e. relationships of earth, sun, and moon) we will gain flexibility- an approach to the art of leaning. Direct living (discussed in Chapter 6) is a realistic attempt at relating to the guidance of the movement of the spheres rather than interdogmatic time and systems. Direct living is a tangible step toward the art of leaning.

159

Viewing Humanity As A Whole

Viewing humanity as a whole can be compared to the overview one has of a plant from seed to fruition to death. Because one has an overview of the processes of the plant, one knows the complete nature of the plant. One can perceive a seedling and thus project fruition. This kind of over view with respect to humanity allows us to actually project the results of our leaning before they happen. This results in knowing the future.

We must be aware that our individual selves are "equivalent" to the various cells in the leaning plant which were involved in miniscule expansions and/or contractions that ultimately, through *timeless persistence,* resulted in the eventual "lean" of the plant. Spherical vision will allow us to realize the wholeness of humanity. If we relate to the wholeness (the unity) of *humanity,* we begin to know the *nature* of the whole of humanity. Knowing the nature of something gives one a certain knowledge of the future with respect to that thing. An example is, again, the banana plant. I know the nature of the plant to lean toward the light. I rotated it around so it leans against the wall. Now I know a certain aspect of its future. It will lean toward the light again.

The more we expand our scope of vision, the more we know about the nature of things, thus, the more we know about the future.

Let's say the scope of our vision is the circle opposite. We see ourselves with a problem- a "bummer." The bummer is coming at us from the front and we must decide how to adapt or deal with it, knowing only what we know from our scope of vision. We don't know where the real source of the bummer is. Our scope of vision is not yet that expansive. We only know from what direction it appears to be coming.

In this diagram, we have expanded our scope of vision. We see the bummer coming from behind us instead of from the front. By expanding our scope of vision, we gained a better understanding of it. We know it appeared to be coming from in front of us, only due to our narrow scope of vision. We still do not know the source of the bummer, but our method of adaption or dealing with it will be different now that we know it is not coming from in front of us.

We have again increased the scope of our vision. Now we see the source of the bummer. Now we know very much about how to adapt to this dilemma. Our adaptation will most likely be much more appropriate now that we know the source of the problem. Expanded vision (a step toward spherical vision) can show us the nature of humanity as a whole. Knowing the nature of humanity over large blocks of natural time (movement of the spheres) can give us insight into our future. It can also direct conscious evolution.

Being adept at the art of leaning demands expanded (and eventually spherical) vision. *Seeing* (if we don't block what we see) will bring forth leaning. Just like the rising sun brings us the morning- seeing brings leaning. Understanding leaning is: recognizing, through blocks of natural time and the "wholeness" of humanity, the tiny steps that build up to actual movement. This movement represents flexibility, adaptation, and evolution. It can be conscious or unconscious.

Tiny steps, inspired by vision, are a beginning. Giant steps often have traumatic effects which can enhance the condition of rigidity. A good example of this is the radical counter cultural movement of the late 60's and early 70's when the hippies came running from the cities to the southwest and radically changed their lives by living off the land in the mountains there. This was a giant step. They made a great statement but the trauma of roughing it was ultimately too much for their inherent rigidity. Emotionally, physically and spiritually, it was too big a step. Consequently, most of those original hippies have slipped back into the mainstream of the swarm of humanity they were trying to escape. The point here is that tiny steps are *sure* steps. The banana plant made tiny unnoticeable steps toward the light. This is leaning.

Looking back into time (prehistoric, early earth) and out into the universe can further facilitate a grasp of the concept of leaning inspired and directed by spherical vision. Spherical vision is ultimately an *interaction* with what is being perceived and eventually an interaction with all that is. Now, to interact with something, one must first include it in his/her reality. This brings up a big issue- inclusion and exclusion.

Inclusion and Exclusion

Many (or most, or all) of us, due to boundaries drawn by our egos, choose to exclude certain people and things (and phenomenon) from our accepted reality. For instance, the black people have been excluded in the past by the white people; the Jews have been excluded by the Germans; the natural processes of the earth have been excluded from modern life styles; dark has been excluded from light; etc. etc. Wolfgang Pauli, a well known physicist, brought forth an interesting principle regarding the electron (the particle wave that swarms around the nucleus of an atom of which we are all made). It is called the principle of exclusion. It puts forth that no electron may enter into a state (place and condition) already occupied by another electron. This fact can be projected into individual persons, animals and plants, since all are made of electrons. Thus we have a tendency to exclude, based on electron activity in our body/brain makeup. However, this "desire" of the electron to be in a state of its own is basically what allows atoms to interact and change their nature (i.e. make other elements) due to the fact that electrons move (they actually leap) from state to state and from atom to atom in the process of chemical and electronic activity in matter. This activity is the basis for all that is. Thus this principle of exclusion paradoxically gives us both ego and our ability to merge. **We have to be something before we can merge with something.** What this amounts to is: Yes, we have a tendency, due to the nature of the elementary parts that make us up, to exclude- and exclude we do. However, if we can look further than exclusion, we find merger. This means that *inclusion* is understood (so to speak) in an overview of the *exclusion* process. In other words, the principle of exclusion is what makes the electron an "individual" capable of inclusion. The electron consequently includes and interacts with anything in the universe. It is a "free body" in the universe.

We too, can be free bodies in the universe- first through development and acceptance of our egos (both individually and collectively) and then to advance to total inclusion of all that is in this ego.

Inclusion is the very secret to sustenance (i.e. "everlasting life").This can be written thusly- sustenance is directly proportionate to inclusion. For instance, the universe has been around longer than anything else because in *includes* everything else. The planet earth has been around longer than any species of plant or animal because it *includes* all species of plant and animal. Thus, the more we include, the more we become. The more we become, the broader our range of sustenance. I believe this is a tangible interpretation of the "everlasting life" mentioned in the Bible and in many other religious and mystical texts.

If we look at the contrary of this, we find that various plants and animals (and soon humans?) have become extinct because their realities (and resulting abilities to adapt) did not *include* all the possibilities of geographic and climatic change on the planet. In many cases, this just means inclusion of other plant and animal species that (because of their nature) can affect the ability to cope with those they interact with. An example of this is the modest creosote bush found in the southwest. This bush presently holds the title of the oldest living thing on the planet. It is older than redwoods and older than bristle cone pines, both of which were previously thought to be the oldest living things on the planet. The creosote bush, among many other unique *inclusions*, attracts and includes in its sphere of existence, a certain type of termite who delights at building its underground village full of tunnels directly under the creosote bush. These tunnels take what little water there is, deeper into the ground around the creosote bush, thus, greatly increasing the potential absorption of the plant for any given amount of rain fall. Basically, the *inclusion* of the termites results in irrigation of the plant.

Let's look at the inclusion/exclusion principle in a human situation. You are on a dark and lonely road in the New Mexico mountains. It is winter and the temperature is thirty degrees below zero and you have car trouble. You are completely stalled and in danger of freezing to death. By the way, you are a white person who is prejudiced against black people, i.e. you do not *include* them in your accepted sphere of existence. Well, along comes a black man in a nice warm truck and offers you a ride to the nearest town which is 60 miles away. If you decide to include black people in your reality, you could be saved from freezing to death. If you decide to continue to exclude them, you could die. The point being that if we are of a state of mind to include all possibilities, realities, beings, conditions, etc. (allow them to exist in our reality), we are increasing the wholeness and potential sustenance of ourselves. Thus, the more we include, the

greater our chances of survival as individuals and as a species. This can be projected right on out to all things on the planet and in the universe. The result being an endless participation in everlasting life. Thus, **sustenance is directly proportionate to inclusion.** The electron, as a result of its exclusion, gains enough individuality to then include and interface with all that is. Thus it experiences everlasting life. We too can experience everlasting life by gaining the strength to *include* all peoples, all animals, all plants, all the planet, all of the solar system, etc., etc. This total inclusion is the result of spherical vision.

Slowly leaning toward total inclusion results in a dilution of the ego. Thus we slowly lean into a beingness, a oneness, with all that is. Through inclusion and spherical vision, we can slowly lean toward a non-local awareness of all that is.

I've been to your space
I've seen how you live
I've been to your heart
I've seen how it gives
I've been over your body
    so smooth so alive
I've been inside your head
I went in through your eyes

You're illusive and dancing
    while revealing your features
And the people that bear them
I call them my teachers
They've come to me holding
    your torch in their hand
When it flickers and dies
I cannot understand

Revelations have hinted
    you'll come from inside
But not till my poisons
    have all burned out or died
I've escaped from the sexes
I've escaped from the stars
I lean toward the sunlight
    and that's what you are.

Perhaps the human condition, as we know it, has human-kind locked outside of a paradise with the male aspect possessing in itself the key and the female aspect intuitively knowing where the door is. Thus nature has it that only wholeness can enter. Man is afraid to include woman in his selfness. Woman is afraid to include man in her selfness. Both aspects attract and repel each other. Evolution would have them become one- ego would have them war. So begins the choice, the chance, and the dance.

CHAPTER SEVEN
NON LOCAL AWARENESS

We have established "The Art of Leaning" as a method to take us to a state of mind from which we can get a grasp of the concept of "non-local awareness." The more the art of leaning is understood and actually applied, the greater our chances of experiencing non-local awareness on something other than just an intellectual level.

Non-local awareness can be called a dance. This is a dance that everything is doing with everything else. If we take the concept of spherical vision and add to it the dimension of time- all time including past, present and future, it will approach non-local awareness. If we take the "object" being observed by spherical vision and make it *all that is,* this approaches non-local awareness. Maneuvering, merging, spherical vision, leaning, and inclusion are all methods of approaching a state of non-local awareness.

A few decades ago when the world's best physicists found themselves in the "arena of mutual participation" (see chapter 4), they stumbled onto something they termed "non-local awareness." Fritof Capra, author and physicist, was the first to point out in his book, **The Tao of Physics**, that mystics in the Far East have been speaking for years about this phenomenon (non-local awareness) that modern science is just stumbling onto from a completely different direction. Any time two vastly different "schools" such as physics and mysticism find themselves in the same arena, we have truly found an unarguable phenomenon worth "riding."

The physicists came across it as they explored the subatomic world and found that matter was, at its lowest common denominator, almost nothing at all. It was in this nothingness that non-local awareness was observed. There is a well known experiment that first revealed non-local awareness to, among others, Albert Einstein. This experiment is known as the Bell Experiment which is discussed in depth in many books about quantum physics. However, it is presented in terms that are difficult for the average person who is not familiar with quantum physics to deal with. I will, therefore, attempt to summarize what the physicists found in terms that do not require a thortough background in that science. A basic understanding of this experiment can provide a grasp of non-local awareness.

Basically, they found that all particles and forces in the subatomic world (i.e. the makeup of the atom) are interrelated. All is in each and each is in all. Specifically, they found that "how and when" one observes a particular phenomenon in the subatomic world, has an effect upon that phenomenon (the observer is actually a participant). We must remember *we* are made up of the subatomic world, thus we are actually trying to observe a dance that we, in fact, are dancing.

The principle of exclusion, discussed in the previous chapter, puts forth that no electron can occupy the same state as another electron. The "state", in the case of this experiment, has to do with the electric charge of the electron which is brought about by the direction of its spin. Therefore, as a result of the exclusion principle, if we have two electrons in a system, and if electron "A" is observed to be spinning up, then electron "B" will be spinning down, since it can't be in the same state as "A". However, electron "A" does not always react in relation to the observer/participant with the same direction of spin. This, in turn results in electron "B" "knowing" the direction of spin of electron "A", and consequently, has been found to spin in the opposite direction. This "knowing" takes place no matter what the distance between the electrons is- be it .0002 inch or 2000 miles. The effect is instantaneous. This is found *not* to be a message transfer even at the speed of light. It is an inherent "knowing", not a communication but rather a *non-local awareness.*

Physicists have known about non-local awareness for years, but what it means relative to the current human condition and how to wedge it into our already rigid reality, are questions they have not been able to answer at this point. Mystics have alluded to the "all knowingness" in many of their experiences for centuries, but they have not really been able or willing to put it "out there" in such a way that the average unadept person could relate to it as an aspect of his/her everyday life. The teachings of the Bible even refer to this phenomenon when they say God is in "all places at all times." This kind of statement, up until now, has been deemed rather abstract and, at best, available only to God. However, it is beginning to appear more "real" and available to us now that modern physics, ancient mysticism and traditional religion all seem to be unfolding the same story.

I believe, since we are made up of electrons, this phenomenon, this ability, they have to be "non-locally aware," is available to *us*. We are, however, currently asleep to this knowledge. Carl Jung speaks of something he calls 'syncronosity'. This is *"knowing"* someone was coming or *"knowing"* something was happening somewhere without knowing where this information came from. Most of us as humans have experienced this a few times in our lives. Synchronicity is an indication that non-local awareness is available to us if we want to look for it. Recent brain research has led us to the "right brain and left brain" discovery, whereby, the left brain is more concerned with logic and the right brain is more concerned with intuition. They are linked by a small "bridge" called the corpus callosum, which, if severed, reveals the difference, or individuality of the two brains. Many straight-forward experiments have illustrated a conflict between the two brains when the synthesizing affect of the corpus callosum is absent.

Modern day living patterns (i.e. dogmas) really call upon the left brain logic much more than the right brain intuition. This is apparent when we observe that male energy is commonly associated with logic and female energy with intuition, and we live in a male dominated society. The point here is, that as a society, our lack of balance between male and female energy, which is associated with our lack of balance between left and right brain use, leaves us in a condition where we are basically not *including* a very important aspect of ourselves in our "accepted reality." Therefore, we are, in effect, *excluding* phenomenon such as non-local awareness from our reality. So it stands to reason that "inclusion", as discussed in the previous chapter, is one of the first steps toward a non-local awareness. In this case, it is inclusion of right brain, inclusion of female energy and inclusion of intuition. Our *exclusion* of these principles renders us inert, thus our general lack of maneuverability. The electron not only includes the opposite electrical charge in its "reality," *it can become the opposite electrical charge.* That is to say, any electron is capable of either an up or a down "spin-state." It is this maneuverability of the electron that renders it whole and thus non-locally aware of all the parts of the whole. *Inclusion and maneuverability between poles can also render us whole and thus non-locally aware.*

We have found for ourselves a polar reality- positive and negative, male and female, right and left, good and bad, dark and light, etc. We have a certain tendancy to *exclude* one half of each of these polar pairs through definitions put forth in our accepted dogma. If we fully *include* and accept *both* aspects of these various "spin-states" (in electron language) we will become whole. This wholeness, as it expands, will shatter every crystalized dogma that stands between us and the God who is "in all places at all times", the "all knowingness" -the "non-local awareness."

Dancing

To include the opposite aspects of a polarized reality is like dancing with death. It takes openness, sensitivity, and guts. Dancing with death is radically different than seeking death or resisting death. *It is the inclusion of death that makes one capable of dancing with it.* Death is simply the polar opposite of life, and like all our other dualities, we must include both life and death in our wholeness to really be whole. There is much more to us than just our "life." There is also our death. There is a dance between two electrons of opposite charge, each with the capacity to "be" the other. Likewise, there is a dance between life and death. Each has a capacity to "be" the other. Non-local awareness exists as a result of this dance. We cannot simply be one of the partners in the dance and experience non-local awareness. Furthermore, we cannot experience non-local awareness by being both partners. We must "become" the dance itself.

The journey from an individual, insecure, highly polarized human being to the "becoming" of a dance between energy and matter- between life and death, is indeed, an awesome one. The art of leaning is a path. Spherical vision can illuminate the way. Maneuvering, merging, inclusion, and expansion are "dynamic steps of the dance", but again, it is the becoming of the dance itself that results in non-local awareness. This means that non-local awareness is simply not available to a polarized human being. Constant conscious application of the various "dynamic steps of the dance" will eventually result in a de-polarization, which is the beginning of wholeness. This wholeness is fundamentally a state of mind. The physical condition that follows is simply a manifestation of that state of mind. In other words, *once humankind attains a state of mind that is whole, the physical manifestation of that wholeness will be entirely different than the physical manifestation of polarization that presently prevails.* Therefore, as we move toward a non-local awareness, we will move out of the human condition as we know it. The question is; are we too attached to the human condition to do this?

We can begin to dilute our attachment to the human condition by observing the wholeness and the dancing that has already been going on in our environment. We can thereby recognize that we are but a small part of a wholeness that will go on with or without humans. This fact just might provide us with the humility we need to begin the journey.

Long ago, the earth was covered with what has been called the "primordial soup." The atmosphere of the earth was radically different then, with almost no oxygen. We wouldn't have existed. A simple form of algae had evolved and was growing without anything eating it or competing with it in any way. Soon, the story goes, the primordial soup all over the earth was filled with this algae that took in carbon dioxide and put out oxygen. The oxygen was basically a pollutant to the carbon dioxide atmosphere that supported the algae. The algae proliferated unchecked for so long that the oxygen level of the atmosphere reached a critical level for the algae. The waste product of the algae, oxygen, was "polluting" it out of existence. Does this sound familiar? Strangely enough, right at this time of crisis, animals began to evolve. They just happened to breathe in oxygen and breathe out carbon dioxide. Thus, one of the many dances of earthly existence began and is still going on today. This is the dance between animals and plants, each one breathing out what the other breathes in and each breathing in what the other breathes out. Plants provide the oxygen in the atmosphere for us to breathe. They are part of the whole picture of our existence. They are part of us and we are part of them.

Every breath we take is an exchange with plants. If we realize our connections with our immediate environment, we will tend to include it more as an aspect of ourselves. This is called *local awareness*. Local awareness provides a graphic tangible model of the much more expansive "non-local awareness." Humankind is, at this point, a failure at local awareness; or maybe we are successful because we have learned by doing all the wrong things. At any rate, this obviously puts non-local awareness completely out of reach from our present state of mind. However, *local awareness*, if acquired, can stretch to non-local awareness the way success stretches to confidence. The magic is the same.

Local awareness is recognizing the wholeness and the interrelatedness of all that exists on the planet. There was some "consciousness" (the wizard energy) that evolved animals to balance out the critical oxygen level crises of the algae long ago. We are in a similar situation now with our various human wastes and pollutants in the atmosphere and the waters of our planet. Conscious evolution would have us do something to maintain the balance, i.e. to *dance* with our garbage - recycle it and/or transform it like the animals transformed the oxygen back to carbon dioxide for the algae, and later other plants, to thrive on.

Nature creates these dances and one of them just happened to include us. Conscious evolution would have us now create our own dances with nature. We can orchestrate these dances as a result of a local awareness. Local awareness is a tangible opportunity to use the same "steps of the dance" (maneuvering, merging, inclusion, and expansion) that will eventually lead us to non-local awareness. The art of leaning can be used as a "way," and spherical vision can be used as an illumination of that way. In other words, learning to live and dance with the processes of this planet is but an exercise in techniques used eventually to transcend the planet. "We will only enter the heavens through the earth."

Essence Relating

A good way to lean toward an understanding of non-local awareness is to continue to explore local awareness. Let's look at a tree, a horse, and a human. These creatures are all potentially within the realm of our local awareness, although sometimes we are not aware of anything but ourselves. Being alive, these creatures all have life in common. We relate to them relative to their surface form. Rarely do we penetrate beyond it. If we did, we would reach a common denominator that could be called essence. This common denominator is "physically real" because all three living things are, in their lowest molecular breakdown, made up of the DNA molecule which is a product of the carbon atom. So there is a basic common essence to all living things. Of course, the carbon atom also has much in common with all other atoms, thus we have a basic common essence of all things. The point here is, there are *various levels of essence* one can relate to as opposed to simply relating to the surface image of all one sees. Essence relating takes us deeper into what we are relating to. Essence relating is a facet of merging. *Those who are adept at essence relating go straight through dogmas, egos, fears, and brick walls. Their ability to penetrate is matched by their ability to be penetrated.* Essence relating is truly an interaction.

We can make a graphic analogy of essence relating to help make the intellectual concept a tangible possibility. Let's take the three figures of the tree, the horse, and the human, and imagine they are made of wax. Each of these figures has a tiny quartz crystal inside. (Quartz crystal has a certain vibration which is why it is used to power small clocks, watches, crystal radios, etc.) Now, imagine how you would relate to each of these wax figures based on their surface image, i.e. their form. (Figure 1) You are not relating to their essence, the crystal vibration inside, you are only relating to surface form. The appearance of the surface form actually dictates your reaction. This is usually the case in our reality. We don't relate, we react. Our reactions are based on the surface of the form. The three different forms dictate three different reactions. Then, if the individual figures are beautiful, healthy, friendly, ugly, etc., these different conditions of the form further complicate but still dictate our reaction.

Now let's imagine a great increase in temperature and the wax figures begin to melt. (Figure 2)

As the surface of the forms begin to change, we discover we weren't really relating to them- we were only reacting, because we find our reactions are changed by the changing form. True interactive essence relating doesn't change with the form; it is constant regardless of the surface form. As the temperature increases and all the forms melt into blobs, (Figure 3) we are appalled and repelled because these blobs do not fit our interdogmatic images of what these creatures should be. We learn something else- that is, most of our reactions themselves simply come from inter-dogmatic, and inter-ego projections. So, we do not know how to relate. We simply react, and our reactions themselves are not from what is out there but rather from what we *project* out there.

Now the temperature continues to rise and all the wax melts away. (Figure 4) There is nothing left but four identical vibrating crystals unchanged by the temperature.

In our analogy, these crystals were the "essence" of the wax forms. If we were involved in essence relating in the first place, we would have penetrated all three figures down to an essence level and found their quality and equality. We could have then related to this essence through all the temperature variations and found no change in our interaction with it throughout the changes in form. *This is called a "stable interaction" and there is much power here.*

The analogy suggests we avoid *reaction* completely, and learn to relate on an essence level to experience "stable interaction." Stable interaction is *local awareness* and a giant step toward *non-local awareness*. The key here is in finding the essence of other living things and eventually *all* other things, both living and non-living. I submit that if we simply find the essence in ourselves, our energy band, we will know where to look for it in other things. Finding our own essence will automatically tune us in to the essence of other things the same way being quiet allows us to hear the singing of the birds. We must begin living on an essence level to relate on an essence level. (See page 12 sustenance = essence.)

This calls for the inclusion of all things into the network of ones sensory perception, as essence *is not singular.* The essence of life for example, includes the tree, the horse, and the human. The essence of matter includes all that is. Relating and living on an essence level begins with the melting of the wax of ones own form. If we learn to relate to our own essence in this way, we will know where to look for essence in the universe. It is the ultimate awareness that the two are the same which will eventually bring us to the realization we are free.

Leaning and Major Leaps

When a child is learning to dive off a diving board, it usually *leans* over the edge to a certain critical point where gravity, that organizer of mass, takes over and pulls the child into the water. Without the initial leaning on the part of the child, gravity never would have pulled it into the water.

The child, through leaning, set itself up for a natural force to take over and bring about a "major leap" in its life- its first leap into water. Likewise, humanity can lean toward a certain realm, such as non-local awareness, and set itself up for a natural phenomenon to take over and bring about a major leap in its evolution. In this case the natural phenomenon is consciousness, the organizer of energy.

Both leaning and major leaps are factors that go hand in hand in the process of evolution. The following quotation from a National Geographic article by Kenneth F. Weaver entitled "The Search for Our Ancestors" is scientific verification of this:

> "Just how evolution works is the subject of much discussion among today's biologists. One idea is that evolution is gradually taking place all the time, (leaning) because of mutations and changing environmental influences. Another proposal is that long periods of relative evolutionary stability are punctuated by sudden appearances of new species, (major leaps). This hypothesis is called punctuated equilibrium. It may well be, many scientists say, that both kinds of evolution are in operation."

This is much like the critical mass theory in physics when something reaches a critical point where it changes form and/or position. The "critical point" observation lends impetus to the act of leaning. Leaning itself is sometimes too slow to provide enough visible change to encourage the leaner. However, knowledge of the critical point that can (as a result of leaning) literally take us the rest of the way, underscores the power of leaning. It is like hitching a ride on a natural phenomenon. We would never catch this ride if we never leaned toward it. Few are the children who simply leap without leaning into the waters of continuous evolution. If we are to "make the leap," we must lean and solicit unarguable phenomenon, (natural forces) to give us that "free" ride. Leaning simply puts us in a position to catch this ride.

If you do not lean, gravity will not take you...
God will not either.

With this in mind, continued ever-expanding local awareness is the immediately tangible leaning process that will place us in position for the leap into non-local awareness. Let's look at another example of *local awareness* as it boarders the realm of *non-local awareness*. This is a place near that critical point where we make the leap.

Imagine that you own a fairly delicate potted plant that cannot handle very intense sunlight. If placed in intense sunlight, it simply shrivels and dies. It is cloudy and you are leaving your house for work. The weatherman predicts clouds all day, so you set your potted plant on the window sill of an open window for some fresh air and maybe a bit of gentle rain. You have had this plant for some time and are aware that it produces beautiful fragrant blossoms. In the past you have mistakenly left it in the sun and observed it begin to shrivel. You have also seen how well and "happy" it is in the shady spot with lots of water, and you have seen and enjoyed its many fragrant blossoms. Thus you have an attachment and more than that, a relationship with this plant. You have included it in your sphere of awareness. It has made its needs and its gifts known to you and you have accepted both into your selfness. Unlike a more complicated human relationship, you have no blocks in relating to the plant because it simply responds to what you give it in a most predictable way without any "trips" of its own. It is clear and honest about its needs and its gifts.

Now you have left your house on this cloudy day with the plant on an open window sill. As is quite often the case, the weatherman was wrong, the clouds totally dissipate and the sun comes out bright and strong. You are far on the other side of town but you "see" the sun is out all over the valley. You feel it on your skin and you see it with your eyes. In the same instant you feel the warmth of the sun on your skin, you "know" instantaneously that your plant is shriveling up. There was no actual communication from the plant to you but because the essence of the plant has been included in your sphere of consciousness, you *know* it is dying. Therefore, you *know* what is going on in another place because of the inclusion of a living thing which is in that place into your sphere of consciousness. This is an experience of local awareness as it approaches non-local awareness. It is not fully non-local because you physically saw the sun was shining on you and the plant at the same time. (You saw both you and the plant subjected to the same stimuli.) However, without physically seeing the plant, you knew what it was doing because it had been included in your sphere of consciousness.

The principle of local awareness means including things, people, the earth or whatever you choose into your sphere of consciousness; or a better way of saying it, expanding ones sphere of consciousness to include, without discrimination, all things. This must be done slowly. This is the slow *lean* toward a critical point where the "gravity" of another level of consciousness will pull you over into it- a major leap. Small steps (slow leaning) are rarely lost because they represent a growth process. Giant steps are like bending the plant. The growth process gives the small steps more "mass" than giant steps which leave a lot of "untrodden ground" between them.

Consequently this "untrodden ground" is not tangibly included. It is only intellectually included and this is not enough to get it to the "critical point." The only real giant step that can be taken, (the major leap) must be taken in alignment, (hand in hand) with a natural phenomenon, such as a child "riding" gravity shown in the previous example. Thus, energy riding facilitates major leaps. "The leaning" is the aligning of ones self with the current. "The leap" occurs when the current takes you. It is this alchemy of movement that brings about the "quantum leaps" in evolution which bring us closer and closer to God. Constant leaning toward universal vision, the current of evolution- the energy band, is what puts us in position to make these leaps.

Expansion

The major difference between our leaning and that of the banana plant in the previous chapter is that the plant leans in one direction and we must lean in all directions at once. This expanding in all directions at once is much like the expansion of the universe that has been taking place since the big bang, if we assume the big bang theory is correct. In this respect, we are indeed models of the universe in which we live.

WE ARE MEANT TO ALIGN OURSELVES WITH THE EXPANDING UNIVERSE AND ACTUALLY RIDE THE PHENOMENON OF IT. NOW THAT WE ARE QUITE SURE THE UNIVERSE IS INDEED EXPANDING, OUR RIDING OF THIS PHENOMENON COULD IN ITSELF REVEAL WHAT WE LONG TO KNOW ABOUT THE UNIVERSE- WHERE IT CAME FROM AND WHERE IT IS GOING. THIS IS THE WAY OF THE WIZARD- TO ALIGN WITH AN UNARGUABLE PHENOMENON, RIDE IT AND THEN SIMPLY EXAMINE ONES SELF TO THEREBY UNDERSTAND THE PREVIOUSLY NOT UNDERSTOOD PHENOMENON.

To fully understand a frog,
you must *become* a frog.

Expansion, the art of leaning in all directions at once, can be examined graphically to enlighten us about the various obstacles or "blocks" that might present themselves to the expanding entity.

This diagram illustrates an expanding sphere with various blocks surrounding it. The expanding sphere represents the expanding human consciousness. Notice that when the sphere is small in relation to the spaces between the blocks, there are obviously less blocks to encounter.

When the sphere becomes larger in relation to the spaces between the blocks, more blocks are encountered. The greater the consciousness, the more obstacles there are to keep it from getting still greater, whereas, a tiny "sphere" of consciousness can expand quite a bit without encountering even a single block. I wish to suggest that human consciousness (the sphere) expands only as far as the nearest block. If one block is in the way on one side of the sphere, the whole sphere is stopped from further expansion because consciousness is an all inclusive, pure wholeness. It does not simply expand on the side away from the block nor does it expand around the block. The block, wherever it occurs, "stops" or switches off or terminates expansion until the block is dissolved. The broader the expansion, the more possible blocks. This results in a radical slowing down of expansion as the sphere gets larger. Keep in mind the sphere is really a multidimensional expansion, far beyond a simple sphere.

We must also remember at any given point, we can experience a "major leap" in this expansion process. This major leap would further facilitate expansion and consequently additional shifts or leaps. However, in between the leaps, *the on-going multi-directional leaning or expansion is necessary to keep one (species, individual, etc.) constantly maneuvering into a position to make another evolutionary leap.* Thus we can consciously bring about or participate in our own evolution. The instant we stop leaning, (expanding) we have all but eliminated our chances for a leap, thus bringing our evolution to a halt. The universe will simply go on without "us."

Among other things, this analogy shows us that dissolving the blocks is a major issue in the continuing growth or evolution of humankind. These blocks can be dogmas, prejudices, judgments, fears, limits of language, etc. In order to present a model for dissolving these blocks, we will look at that more tangible "relative" of consciousness called gravity. (A discussion of the relationship between gravity and consciousness is held in chapter 1, page 4). Gravity itself remains unclear even to modern physicists, but the following explanation will stand on the shoulders of modern physics and step from there to the "peaks" of intuition.

Gravity- A Result of Mass

Gravity is an organizer of mass. Objects of mass, "experience" gravity. The greater the mass and density, the greater the gravity. The diagram opposite illustrates a two-dimensional concept of the principle of gravity. We have a steel ball placed between two 1" wide rubber bands stretched between point A and point B. Notice the rubber bands are slightly stretched and displaced by the mere existence of the steel ball. Figure 2 shows the steel ball growing in size. The more the ball grows, (greater mass) the more tightly it stretches the rubber bands- thus more pressure is placed on the ball by the increased tension, i.e. the greater the mass the greater the gravity.

In this analogy the steel ball represents matter and the rubber band represents that void or condition out of which matter is formed. In the words of modern physics, nothing exists in it but anything can "appear" at any time. Nothing is here but *everything* is potentially here. The materialization of something (matter) creates a pressure against this "void of potentiality." The larger and more dense the materialized object- the greater the pressure, thus we have gravity. This analogy must be projected into three dimensions, a condition where the ball has manifested in a block of rubber for example. The very existence of the ball results in a pressure on the ball. (See diagram on next page.)

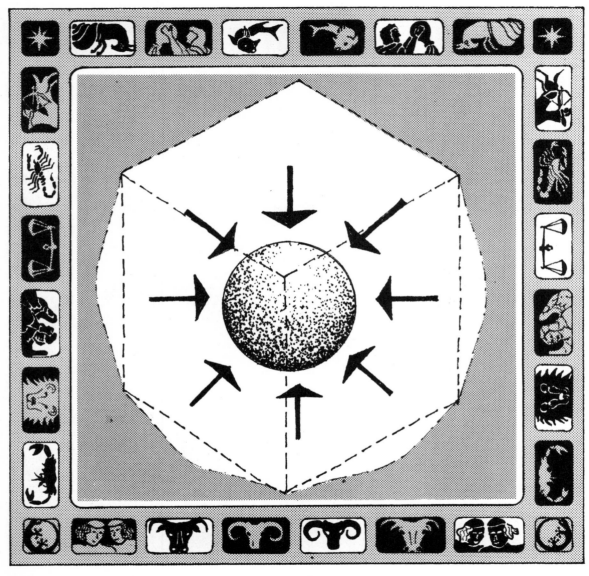

Gravity- A Result of Density

The reason for constructing this kind of model is to arrive at a simple method of looking at density, which is an aspect of matter. In more dense matter, the atoms are more tightly packed and in less dense matter they are less tightly packed. There is more space or actually more of the void of potentially *within the matter itself.* This suggests that all matter has some of the void of potentiality within it, i.e., there is a certain *interpenetrating of matter and the void of potentiality.* This in turn suggests matter is but a condensation of the void of potentiality. As density of matter increases, (as atoms become more tightly packed) the void of potentiality is allowed to penetrate the matter less and less. Obviously, the less the interpenetrating between matter and the void of potentiality, the more tension or pressure will occur, i.e., the more gravity. (See diagram on opposite page.)

Consequently the void of potentiality actually penetrates less dense matter more and mixes with it to some extent, thus reducing the pressure, (gravity) on the mass. Thus we have the modern physicists knowledge of the greater the density of mass, the greater the gravity.

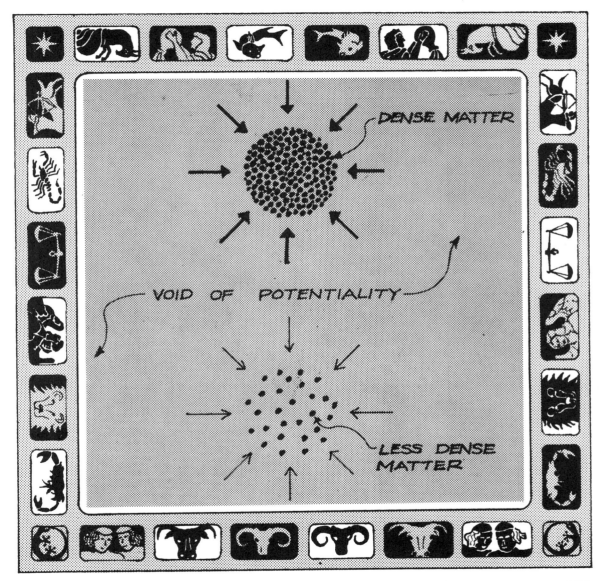

DENSE MATTER

VOID OF POTENTIALITY

LESS DENSE MATTER

JUST AS IT IS THE LACK OF DENSITY IN MATTER THAT ALLOWS IT TO ABSORB AND BE ABSORBED BY THE VOID OF POTENTIALITY, IT IS THE LACK OF DENSITY IN OUR SELFNESS, (OUR REALITY OR EGO, BOTH INDIVIDUAL AND COLLECTIVE) THAT ALLOWS US TO ABSORB OR BE ABSORBED BY THE VARIOUS BLOCKS THAT OBSTRUCT THE EXPANSION OF OUR CONSCIOUSNESS. THE DISCUSSION OF CONSCIOUSNESS IN THE BEGINNING OF CHAPTER TWO OUTLINED THREE FORMS OF CONSCIOUSNESS: HUMAN, LIFE, AND ANGEL CONSCIOUSNESS. OF THESE THREE, HUMAN CONSCIOUSNESS IS THE MOST DENSE, WITH ANGEL CONSCIOUSNESS BEING THE LEAST DENSE. THEREFORE, A LESS DENSE FORM OF CONSCIOUSNESS ALLOWS MORE INTERPENETRATING BETWEEN "US" AND OUR VARIOUS BLOCKS. THIS MAKES FOR LESS RESISTANCE TO EXPANSION. WE FIND HERE **IT IS REALLY *OURSELVES*, NOT OUR BLOCKS, THAT MUST BE DISSOLVED TO ALLOW CONTINUOUS MOVEMENT AND EXPANSION THROUGH THE UNIVERSE.** THE RELATIONSHIP BETWEEN MATTER AND THE VOID OF POTENTIALITY, THE INTERPENETRATING, THE WHAT IS AND WHAT ISN'T, RESULTS IN THE PHENOMENON OF GRAVITY. THE RELATIONSHIP BETWEEN LIFE AND GOD, THE INTERPENETRATING, THE WHAT IS AND WHAT ISN'T, RESULTS IN THE PHENOMENON OF CONSCIOUSNESS.

We consciously give up our density, ourselves, to expand. As we become less dense, we become more locally aware. As we become even less dense, we become non-locally aware. As we become even less dense, we cease to exist- we have consciously come home to God.

Density

If we were to construct a scale model of an atom, the nucleus would be the size of a cherry in the middle of St. Peter's Dome in Rome and the electrons would be orbiting, or swarming, in a rough orbit the size of the dome itself which is 140 feet in diameter. The void or "space" between the cherry and the dome is the void of potentiality as it "exists" within or penetrates the atom or as the components of the atom "exist" within the void of potentiality. This illustrates the interpenetrating of the void and the atom, the common denominator of matter. This interpenetrating is a fundamental attitude of the universe.

In some forms of matter, the atoms are packed together very tightly, thus squeezing the electrons into a closer orbit and reducing the "volume" of the void within the atom. The density is greater. So it stands to reason there must be different "conditions" of matter with respect to density. Greater density usually results in less interaction and more pressure, tension and heat.

There are also different "conditions" available to humanity with respect to density. The greater the density of our ego, our collective dogma, our definition of self, the less interaction and the more pressure, tension and heat. Our density is a state of mind that can become less dense by choice- the choice to lean into a less dense condition. The basic result of this choice is the ability to dilute and eventually evaporate oneself. Thus begins the process of learning to die before we die. This evaporation or dissolving allows us to pass through and interact with the obstacles that block our expansion. It also allows us to interact with the void of potentiality (the matrix). The act of becoming less and less dense, allows expansion through blocks and into the void. Thus we slowly expand, include and become included in, all that is, much in the same way cream when poured into coffee includes and is included in the cup of coffee. We simply give up our defined position, our "localness" and absorb and are absorbed by both the local and the non-local. Our awareness of this process can lead us to a condition of "non-local awareness."

To experience non-local awareness we must learn to dilute and lose our "local determination." This allows us to enter and become aware of domains that our egos, our dogmas, our bodies, our realities will not allow. An example of this is the way arsenic, an ancient and natural medicine, enters our bodies. If taken in an undiluted, condensed form, it will kill us. However, arsenic finds its way into certain spring waters, mushrooms, and some plants. If consumed by us as an integral and proportionate part of water or mushrooms, it becomes a welcome purifier and medicine. Thus, by observing that the dilution of a poison allows itentrance into our bodies, we can project the experience that the dilution of ourselves allows us entrance into otherwise unavailable or inpenetrable domains. This dilution process becomes a principle of expansion as it is the key to passing through our various blocks and eventually out of the human condition altogether. It is from somewhere beyond the human condition that non-local awareness will prevail.

CHAPTER EIGHT
IMAGES OF GOD

Now, let us assume we have acquired the ability to reduce our density, i.e. dissolve ourselves (our egos), and pass through those emotional and dogmatic "blocks" that hinder further expansion. We can now, without obstructions, explore the real potentials of expansion. We must, however, develop a model for this exploration.

Let's imagine a movie projector projecting a film. (See diagram opposite). Light is projected through the film and onto a screen. Likewise, energy is projected through consciousness and onto a "condensation of matter" in the universe. Consciousness organizes energy as a film organizes light.[1] The film, however, is only two dimensional with the illusion of depth. Consciousness is multi-dimensional with the illusion of death. Just as the "organized light" of the film interacts with a white screen and transforms it into what we call a "movie", organized energy interacts with matter and transforms it. This is evolution. Evolution is the process of organized energy interacting with matter, thus "driving" that matter back to energy via various transformations. Evolution moves us toward God.

The result of light organized by a film and then interacting with (projected upon) a screen is a movie. The result of energy organized by consciousness and then interacting with (projected upon) matter is what we call reality. Reality is thus a condensation of matter receiving a projection of consciousness. Just as in a movie house, the projection is "in the air" (so to speak), the "projection" of consciousness is "in" the void of potentiality, i.e. the matrix.[2] Therefore, *any* condensation (of matter or ego) will thus be projected upon just as one holds up a hand in front of the projection in a movie house and gets the *image on their hand.*

Realities are simply condensations in the matrix that "catch" projections.[3] These projections are inherently "in" the matrix. The act of holding up ones hand in a movie house to "catch" a piece of the image of the movie is analogous to the act of matter condensing from the matrix to "catch" a piece of the image of God. Just as the entire reel of film is the "reservoir" of the multitude of images that make up the movie, consciousness itself is the reservoir of the various images of God. This reservoir is what Carl Jung calls the collective unconscious. This is why we see certain aspects of history (both natural and human history) repeating themselves in different ways, from systems to events, symbols, patterns, etc. The projection (energy organized by consciousness) is eternally "there" just waiting for something to project upon. We have here, energy condensing into matter and being organized by gravity. We also have matter evaporating into energy and being organized by consciousness. The organized matter receives the "projection" of the organized energy just as a screen receives the projec-

tion of a film. However, the matrix is itself a multi-dimensional, eternal "projection" of organized energy. Therefore, the very existence of matter is subject to the projection of organized energy. In other words, *the very existence of matter is subject to consciousness.*

This analogy illustrates a pattern, quite possibly the fundamental pattern of the universe. Like all patterns of the universe, we as humans can and do mimic it. We project on to others our images, fears, hopes, dreams, etc. and consequently have those of others projected upon us. Just as in the case with matter (discussed in the previous chapter), our density is a factor in the "effect" of these projections. We basically have a dance of "projecting" and "being projected upon" between matter and energy, between reality and matrix, between human and human, and between human and God.

[1] The organization of energy is introduced on pg 4.

[2] Matrix and void of potentiality illustrate the same idea on pgs. 81-82.

[3] Realities as condensations of the matrix are discussed on pgs. 87-88.

Non-local awareness is a result of *fully* taking part in both aspects of this dance. It is, therefore, not available to us as long as we are confined to specific reality alone. We must take part in the dance between matrix and reality to experience non-local awareness. Eventually, we all take part in the dance when we die. However, to realize non-local awareness in our physical life span, *we must dance before we die.*

Every aspect of this diagram has two labels. One label represents what the drawing actually shows and the other label represents its analogous counterpart.

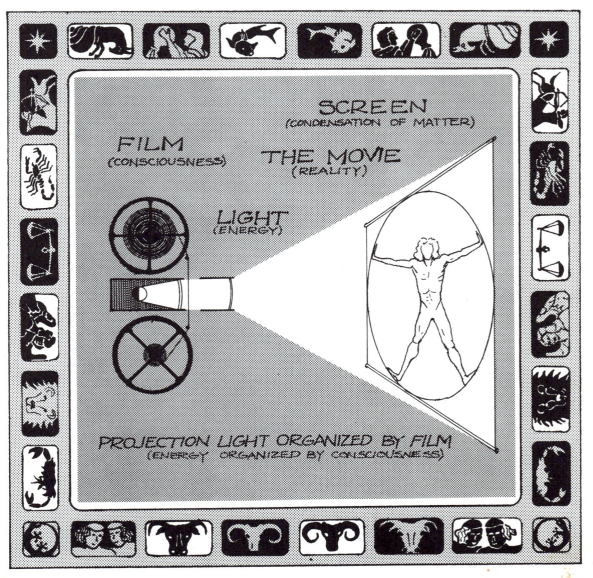

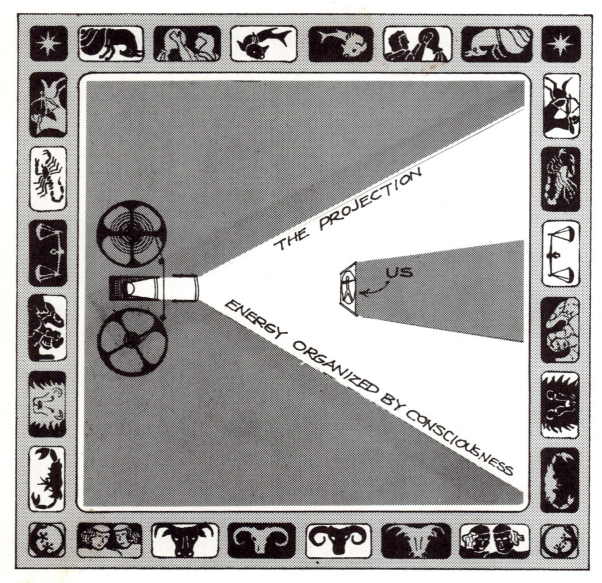

The Transparent Aspect of Expansion

Expansion is actually one of the "steps" to this dance between the "projection" and "that which is being projected upon." To further explore expansion, let's continue with the analogy of the film projector.

In this diagram, we have a tiny screen that only receives a fraction of the full or "whole" picture. This is the position we place ourselves in within the limited language and dogma of "human consciousness." *It is obvious from the way we live on this planet that we just have no idea of what the whole picture is.*

Now, let's say we discover that our tiny little screen is made of thin rubber and we find that we can stretch or expand it. The larger the rubber screen, the more of the whole picture we get. This is the same idea discussed in chapter one (page 8) which states that the greater a space we make for mind, the more mind will fill it. This is how human consciousness grows to become "life consciousness." We have simply ex-expanded enough to "receive" a greater portion of the picture.

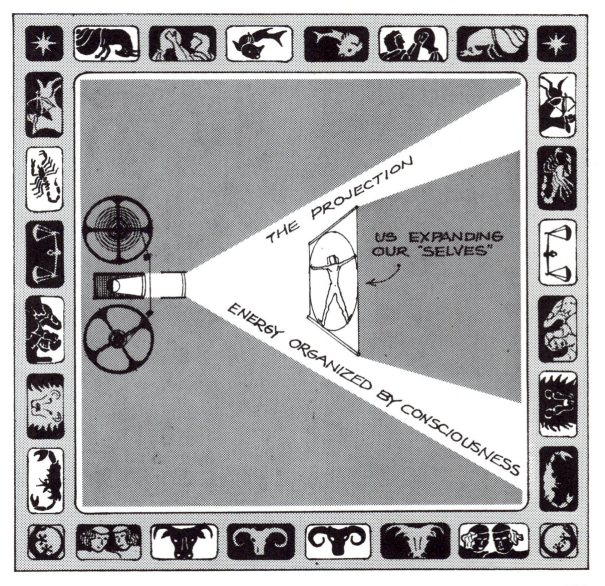

THE PROJECTION

US EXPANDING OUR "SELVES"

ENERGY ORGANIZED BY CONSCIOUSNESS

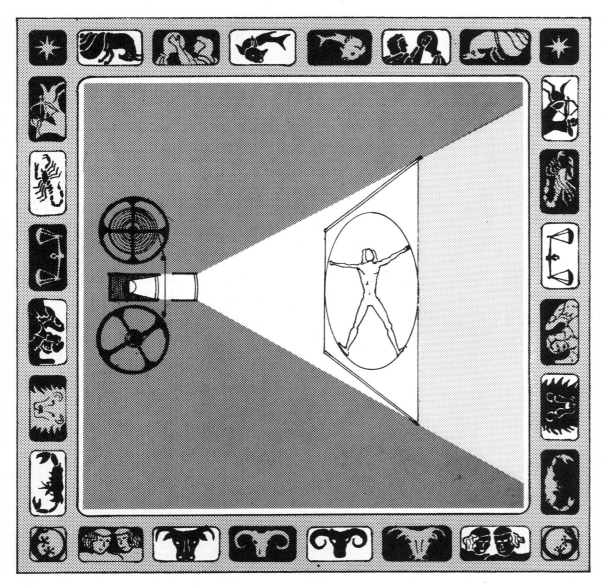

Now let's say we have stretched or expanded the rubber screen to the full size of the projection. We now have a full, whole picture- "angel consciousness",[4] all that is. However, at this stage of the game our rubber screen (because of stretching) has become very thin - so thin that the projection almost passes through it. The screen is approaching transparency. *Transparency is a result of expansion.*

[4] Angel consciousness is discussed in chapter one, pg.4.

195

WE HAVE JOINED THE PROJECTION

To journey beyond angel consciousness, we move the rubber screen back farther and farther from the projector and continue to expand it to keep the full image until it becomes so transparent that it ceases to exist. The projection passes right through it. The rubber screen is us. We can evaporate via expansion, thus "joining" the projection in the void of potentiality.

This is the way consciousness organizes energy and projects it onto matter, thus creating conscious realities, driven or *inspired* by awareness to keep expanding in order to get more and more of the "picture." *When we have lost our inspiration, we have ceased to evolve.* This process of expansion results in transparency and eventual desintigration or evaporation into the all-conscious matrix or void of potentiality. Out of this matrix, matter condenses, thus becoming another "screen" subject to organized energy (the projection of consciousness). This screen is driven by awareness (obtained from the projection of consciousness) to expand and the pattern/cycle/dance continues. Thus expansion is a "step" to the dance of condensation and evaporation of realities. This dance is the pulse of the universe. It is the unarguable phenomenon that encompasses all that is and is not. We can "ride" this phenomenon.

This analogy is only two-dimensional, with humanity as we know it, existing as the "screen" - the first tiny screen. We see from this linear analogy of a multi-dimensional phenomenon that *we* can expand to the point of transparency and eventual evaporation. Thus we become the projection itself (i.e. the matrix) and thereby project onto another "screen" thus driving it to evolution and expansion. "We" actually become the dance itself. This dance is the image of God. We can "be" both aspects of the dance. This is our illusive wholeness which reveals itself to us symbolically in the polarization of our world. Existence as we know it is only *one* aspect of this cycle. The dogma of existence should not (but it does) keep us from "ceasing to exist" as the other aspect of the dance. This ceasing to exist, i.e. learning to die before we die, is another whole aspect of (or step to) the dance. We can, through expansion to the point of transparency, learn to consciously "ride" this phenomenon, thus familiarizing ourselves and identifying our "selves" with both aspects of the dance- reality and matrix. This will open "polar doors", take us to wholeness and show us ourselves as the image of God.

Transcending Time
Now that we see we can be the "projection" as well as "that which is projected upon", let's relate to the freedom and maneuverability this gives us. In the projection itself, we have no reference system, so all the factors that set up our definitions and limitations simply do not exist. Therefore, our definitions and limitations themselves do not exist. We are "in light" when we expand to the point of transparency and become the projection. Time only exists in the "screen" or "projected upon" aspect of the dance. On pages 35 to 38, the mathematical discussion of time puts "us" (our reality) on the future side of the present- not *in* the eternal present. The eternal present *is* the projection aspect of the dance. We do not dwell here, we dwell in the "screen" aspect. In the case of a movie, the screen receives the projection a split second after it is created in the projector because of the finite speed of light. If the organization of light by the film in the projector is considered to be the present, (with regard to the movie) the screen receives the projection a split second in the future, i.e. the screen image exists on the future side of the present.

It takes a split second for the image (the present) to travel from projector to screen. So the screen image happens in the future relative to the projector image.

The organization of energy by consciousness has created an eternal present. But whenever a "screen" (a condensation of matter) appears, it will receive the projection of consciousness in the future compared to the ever-present projection of consciousness existing in the void of potentiality. Thus, as long as we dwell only in the screen aspect of the dance, we will be trapped on the future side of the eternal present, just as a movie screen is always on the future side of the "present" created in the projector.

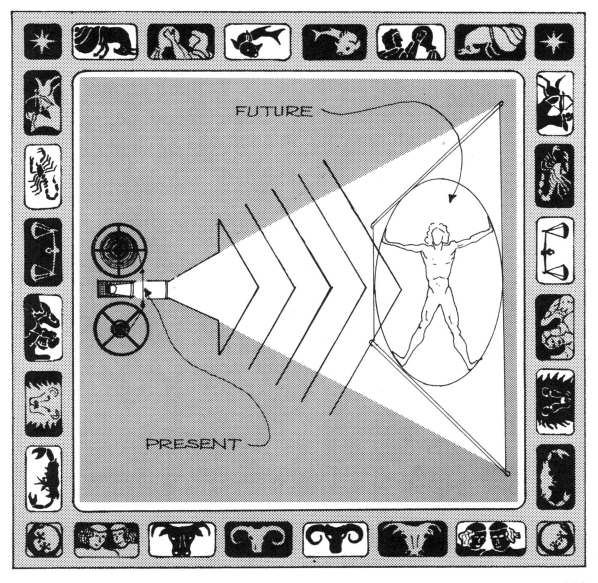

Expansion to the point of transparency will allow us to "see" ourselves in the projection aspect of the dance. This aspect is like a movie projection awaiting a screen. There is nothing tangible here for us to relate to. Therefore, we unfortunately do not relate to this aspect of the dance. Since we are operating from a physical, tangible state, we only relate to tangible concepts. This is like being white and only relating to white people. Our polarization (inability to include anything outside our particular dogma) is our major limitation. This limitation to tangible concepts only, is what keeps us out of the eternal present.

In a movie, the very existence of a screen isolates a "piece" of the projection, thus creating a future and a past relative to that particular "piece" of the movie. Likewise, in our reality, the very existence of matter isolates a "piece" of the ever-existing projection of consciousness, i.e. a "piece" of the eternal present, thus creating a future and a past relative to that particular "piece" of the eternal present.

The light in a projector is organized by the film and thus creates a "present" with respect to the movie. There is no past or future until a piece of this "present" is isolated on a screen. Likewise, energy in the void of potentiality is organized by consciousness and thus creates the eternal present. There is no past or future until a "piece" of this eternal present is isolated on a condensation of matter. The eternal present always is. A future and a past "appear" when a condensation of matter appears and is subjected to this ever-existing projection. This future and past are both relative only to this particular condensation.

If we could simply get to the eternal present, we would know the future. We would know all futures, all presents and all pasts in the eternal present because this is the "place" they all come from. *This is non-local awareness.* Getting to the eternal present is knowing and accepting that we are both the projection and the screen as opposed to only accepting the "screen" aspect of ourselves. Both past and future are just illusions relative to a specific condensation that received projection. This is always going on. It is our limited, isolated "screen" reality that gives us the illusion of a linear sequence in these condensations. Furthermore, most of us only let ourselves "see" one of these condensations at a time. The condensations are infinite; the potential of reality is infinite.

In our current "isolated screen" reality, the present is always slipping away from us. This is like watching a train go past while you are standing by the tracks. The train cars, like the present, slip by and away from you. However, if you

boarded the train or "rode it", the cars would n slip by. There would be no cars on their way you (future) and no cars going away from yo (past). The future and the past would all there with you. Likewise, we can join and "rid the projection through expansion to tran parency. The future and the past, like the tra cars, would then be with us constantly. The tra requires a ticket. Riding the projection al requires a ticket. This ticket is transparency.

Just as we have the option to stand beside t tracks while the train goes by or to ride in it, v also have the option to "be" a condensatio receiving a projection or we can "be" the pr jection. The acceptance of this "dance" betwee "the projection" and "that which receiv projection", and the acceptance that we can "b *both* aspects of this dance, will allow us to begin maneuver back and forth between these tv aspects of ourselves. This is analogous to our fi adventures into right and left brain or our fi adventures into the concept of an opposite s (anima and animus) within ourselves. Consciou free maneuverability between the aspects projection and screen will lend us the overview v need to become our potential- the wholeness the dance itself.

Transcending Existence
Time does not exist outside condensation, reality) nor do we "exist" outside a condensatio Existence, like time, is only relevant to the co densation or screen aspect of the dance just as tl "image" of a movie is only relevant to the screen is projected upon. If there were no screen receive the movie projection, it would simply be long beam of light traveling through space.

Imagine placing little white cards (screens) into this long beam of light at various places. The cards would receive an image- not the complete image, but a piece of it. If you were moving along with the beam of light, you could put a card in and pull it out and then put it back in the same place or some place else in the beam. You would be, in effect, "creating screens" to receive a piece of the projection of the movie just as matter condensing out of the void of potentiality receives a "piece" of the projection of consciousness. With respect to the whole movie, time is only relevant to the card, while the beam of light itself contains all time, i.e. all pasts and futures. The very fact that you place a card in the beam of light makes the card subject to a piece of the movie. The very fact that matter condenses out of the void of potentiality (or matrix), makes this matter subject to the projection of energy organized by consciousness.

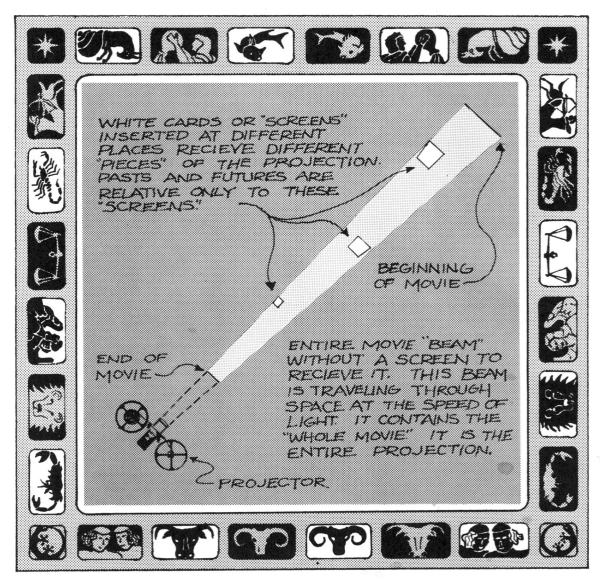

WHITE CARDS OR "SCREENS" INSERTED AT DIFFERENT PLACES RECIEVE DIFFERENT "PIECES" OF THE PROJECTION. PASTS AND FUTURES ARE RELATIVE ONLY TO THESE "SCREENS".

BEGINNING OF MOVIE

END OF MOVIE

ENTIRE MOVIE "BEAM" WITHOUT A SCREEN TO RECIEVE IT. THIS BEAM IS TRAVELING THROUGH SPACE AT THE SPEED OF LIGHT. IT CONTAINS THE "WHOLE MOVIE". IT IS THE ENTIRE PROJECTION.

PROJECTOR

Only within condensed matter, is time or existence (as we know it) a factor. All pasts and futures are "in" the void of potentiality just as they (for the movie) are "in" the long beam of light containing the movie. The very act of placing a card in the beam of light assures us that now there is part of the beam ahead of the card (past) and part of the beam behind the card (future) still to come. However, with no card to isolate such a "reality", neither past nor future are an issue. Likewise, the very act of the material- ization of matter, isolates a reality (a screen) out of the matrix. Relative to this reality, there are futures and pasts with the present always slipping away. With no condensed matter to isolate a reality (i.e. "catch" a projection), past and future are not an issue.

So, we have the void of potentiality analogous to the beam of light containing the movie. We have condensations of matter analogous to the cards (screens) inserted along the beam of light. The screens can come and go while the beam of light always is. Similarly, condensed matter comes and goes while the void of potentiality always is. The void of potentiality contains everything just as the beam of light contains the whole movie. We are like the little cards. We appear and disappear into the light. *When we appear, the light shines on us. When we disappear, we are the light.*

We can (through expansion to transparency) "be" the light. We can dance back and forth between being light and being matter receiving a projection from the light. We are both are aspects. Once we accept this and move with it, we begin to realize that we, in fact, *are* the dance itself. We have only to "ride" this phenomenon to be free, to live, to die, *to be or not to be*- to transcend existence.

The diagram opposite illustrates what we look like when we have transcended existence. The question is - can ego allow us to move in this direction?

Silence is the language spoken
by those who hear
everything.

Nothing is the condition
of that which is
everything.

Wisdom speaks louder
   when it doesn't have to be
   spoken at all.

I can feel its subtle swelling
I can feel its full control
The patterns that it moves in, as yet I do not know
It has a pace- as the ocean's rising tide
It is the father of life- the mother of soul
It's an ever-present force
Infinite Crescendo.

Dissipation beyond all questions and answers how absurd
Fear is just a hubcap- decoration on a wheel
The past is just the future, together they reveal
The structure of the present and the parts your mind conceals
Thoughts have wings like birds flying to and fro
One will someday fly you to
Infinite Crescendo

Stand naked in the sunlight
Release your unborn soul
Let it float around before your eyes
Let it tell you where to go,
It will weave you through the forest of explosive ego mines
You'll simply be on tour, the ghost knows what you'll find
Immune to pain and sorrow
You'll help others carry theirs
Give them your tomorrows, 'cause you can make your own you know
Your strength is ever growing from
Infinite Crescendo.

Allowing Connection

A specific beginning to transcending existence is expansion. A specific step toward expansion is allowing connection. Developing our abilities in this area (with earthly things) provides experience and familiarity with "sensory equipment" that can be used later for "non-local" type connections; specifically, ourselves and the matrix and eventually, ourselves and God.

Imagine a puppet whose limbs are connected to your fingers by strings. When you move a finger, the tight string *instantaneously* pulls up the hand or foot of the puppet. This is not a message at the speed of light- this is simultaneous movement, an instantaneous connection. The string makes the puppet limb "aware" of the movement of your finger. No matter how long the string, the movement of your finger and the puppet's limb takes place simultaneously. Likewise, if the puppet were to move on its own, your finger would "feel" the movement. Feelings are the way we register the energy of other things. It is thru feelings that we become in touch with the rest of the universe.

Now imagine yourself connected to someone else like you are to the puppet. Hands connected to hands and feet connected to feet about ten feet apart. This is a bit scary at first because the "connections" (due to our limited view of things) produce the illusion of a loss of freedom, but alas, *freedom does not come in individual doses.* Therefore, to allow connection, both parties must dissolve their fear of losing freedom because they never really had freedom to begin with. Next, both must realize that both can contribute to whatever movement takes place or one of them can be a "puppet." If both contribute, you must *include* each other into a common sphere of awareness. (close relationships approach this) You each have to become (or acknowledge that you are) different aspects of the same thing. This is where ego appears like a ring of fire, isolating us into fragments of the whole. Ego is just another phenomenon that we must learn to "ride" rather than control or be controlled by. Acceptance of other things as aspects of ourselves leads to *instantaneous connections.* It is through these connections we discover our wholeness. These connections are between human and human, between human and plant or animal, between human and any "thing", between human and matrix or "projection", and between human and God.

205

There is a hand
    that can reach
    through an eye
    to a heart.

It can bring two
    worlds together
    though they be
    far apart.

This diagram symbolically illustrates the dance that begins with "allowing connection." This could be you and your lover, you and your friend, you and the wind, you and a rose, you and the universe, humankind, the earth, etc. We are not separate. . from anything.

We must begin to *allow our connections and live our wholeness.* Our world will blossom. We must give up our separateness to experience wholeness. When we "move our hand" we must know that it affects the entire planet. Just knowing this will make decisions for us. This "knowing" is the gravity that pulls the water down the mountain. There is no decision about which way water flows from the top of a mountain. *Gravity answers all the questions.* Likewise, wholeness answers all the questions relative to our psychic world. Wholeness creates its own gravity. This gravity effortlessly organizes energy the same way the earth's gravity organizes the mountain waters into lakes. Allowing connection on any level is a step toward wholeness and the effortless organization of our energy-alas, no debates, no right or wrong. . . just water flowing down a mountain.

There is a dance that can result from allowing connection between humanity and earth. Chapter five, **Direct Living,** addresses this dance. There is also a dance that can result from allowing connections between humanity and the matrix. There are messages that do not travel, they are instantaneous awareness. We have but to allow connection with the matrix to hear them. We are an aspect of the matrix and it is an aspect of us. There is a dance. The only way to maneuver without misunderstood resistance is to recognize the connection and the unity implied/required. The matrix includes us. We have but to include it to allow the dance to become a conscious part of our being. The matrix unarguably accepts every aspect of us, yet we exclude and negate much about it. Thus we place synchronicity, freedom, and maneuverability (i.e. conscious evolution) out of reach. We are not puppets of evolution, nor can we control evolution. We can, however, consciously participate by allowing connection between us and all that is and between us and all that is not.

We must walk softly on the bridge dear
    that runs between your world and mine
The connections they're not true yet
They have not clearly been defined.

We must respect the venture taken
To hang suspended here in time
Inside our hearts are aching
Outside our lights have ceased to shine.

Now we must know that treading softly
    will never frighten off the beast
But it keeps the bridge from breaking
    while there's nothing underneath.

Soon the spheres of mind and matter
    will have drifted from our view
Then there will be no bridge needed
Both sides of me will lead to you.

We are the
   many faces of
each other.

There is no they. . .
Only other aspect of ourselves.

211

Energy Exchange - Change - Evolution

Allowing connection with and "riding" the patterns of the universe can manifest, project, change or bring about anything we can conceive of within our particular density node or condensation (reality). Indeed, we have manifest our particular reality and with it our bodies, towns, cities, countries, world, solar system, galaxies and universe- depending on the scale at which we are focusing. This also goes for "bodies" at the subatomic level. Through allowing connection (energy exchange) with the matrix, we can *join* power that conceives and manifests. This energy exchange is the "framework" (the pattern) within which we have the potential to exist and to not exist. This is the unchangeable, the unarguable pulse or dance of God. We can destroy other creatures, our planet, ourselves, maybe even someday the solar system; but we cannot destroy this pulse, this dance. This dance will continue with us or without us. The choices are simply relative to the quality of life we have while we do exist. The dance gives us the choice for survival in a living hell or a wonderful paradise. Apparently, many other creatures simply did not have the vision to recognize the dance as an absolute. Therefore, they did not know to allow it, to surrender to it and to ride it to eternity. They resisted, ignored, and perished.

We as humans, have the potential to allow and surrender to this dance. If we reach our full potential, we will "be" the dance. It is the dance itself (not the physical human being which is only an aspect of the dance), that is the image of God. We were created in this image, but our evolution has become so introverted that we currently only relate to the physical aspect of ourselves and tend to think that this physical aspect itself is the image of God. Thus we are confused as to why, if this physical human being is the image of God, it is so limited. *The human condition is but an isolated aspect of the pulsating cosmic dance that, in its wholeness, is the image of God.* In order to further comprehend this dance- this image of God- we can place ourselves in another analogy that takes us close to the process of *being* the dance.

Imagine a vertical walled, box canyon with an infinitely deep river rushing at the bottom. The sheer walls of the canyon are infinitely high. This is a linear analogy because we tend to think in a linear way. It will simply point us in the direction of the truth. Humanity is a creature floating down the canyon on a log.

As far as we can look back we see humanity simply having found the log, holding on to it and floating. Then we see the human climb up on top of the log. Next, he/she works on the log and carves it into a canoe with a paddle. Now the human has acquired some degree of maneuverability. He/she can maneuver from one side of the river to the other. He/she can speed up the already rapid trip down stream or attempt to go against the current but going against the current only slows down the inevitable trip downstream. The human can further "adapt" and ultimately destroy the log in an effort to achieve more ways to resist the stream. He/she can devise ingenious "technological" devices with his/her own body parts and pieces of the log. But the physical resources are obviously limited. (Does this sound familiar?) The human can make itself miserable or comfortable while he/she rides out "life" on the river, but he/she must ride the river or drown. The river doesn't care. The human can destroy itself and/or the log, but he/she can't change the river. The river is the unarguable phenomenon he/she is riding. It is the dance of which the human is but an aspect.

Now let's say the human on the log becomes aware of and accepts and surrenders to the "dance" of the river. As a result of this, his/her energy becomes organized with respect to it. Thus he/she begins to consciously evolve toward a more harmonious condition in relation to the river. Rather than resisting, ignoring or trying to change the river, the human simply surrenders to it and consciously evolves his/her own nature toward that of the river. Lo, the human becomes a fish with gills to breathe in the water and fins to maneuver in it. The human has evolved to a more suitable "form" relative to the phenomenon it has recognized.

Relative to the nature of the river itself, a fish is a much more appropriate "form" than a human on a log. Thus the human is evolving toward its potential. It is now more in tune with the dance of the river. As a fish, the creature gains more insight into the nature of the river because it is much more in tune with it. This gives the creature enhanced vision and allows it to evolve ever more closely to the nature of the river and its dance. It eventually evolves into water itself, thus it becomes the river, it becomes the dance.

First to recognize the dance
Then to allow connection to the dance
Then to maneuver toward the dance
Then to become the dance
Step by step, this is conscious evolution.

We must open our eyes to our dance, accept it, surrender to it and evolve toward it consciously. This is our potential. This is the image of God. Survival for the human on the log was much more difficult than for the fish. Survival for the fish was much more difficult than for the water itself. *Conscious evolution toward the energy patterns that prevail in the universe will allow us to eventually consciously become the universe. Since the universe includes humanity, we will not have lost humanity. . . we will have simply gained the universe.*

If we lean in this direction, there will come a time when the human form is no longer necessary for an "existence." If we do not lean in this direction, there will come a time when the human form can no longer exist. We can recognize the dance or unconsciously cease to exist. The dance does not care. A journey toward the rhythms of the cosmos seems to be on our horizon if we choose to have a horizon. Otherwise we can stay densely defined and introvertedly evolve into a black hole and simply dissappear. This happens in the cosmos as we know it even now.

So, the whole image of God is not available to us in the human form, though our leaning toward it will certainly improve our quality of life while in the human form, as well as improve our chances of completing the conscious journey toward the rhythms of the cosmos.

What we can do now is lean away from the existing introverted evolution and toward the image of God. Direct living is a beginning. Looking, seeing, and leaning are pathways toward direct living and beyond.

Paradise is not at the end of the process. Rather the process itself, if we accept it as such, is paradise. Our resistance to the process and in some cases our ignorance of the process is what keeps us from realizing that we are in paradise. The only thing to resist is the gravity of our own introverted evolution.

Paradise does not exist
unless. . .
This is Paradise.

Archaeological observations indicate there were many awesome civilizations on this planet before us. Many of them had a radically different focus toward life than we do and they seem to have simply disappeared. Did they perhaps get far enough along on the journey toward the rhythms of the cosmos that they ceased to exist in human form? The ways of a human life form even moving close to the rhythms of the cosmos would be awesome for us to behold. Much of the ancient architecture and "art" in Egypt and South America appears so to us now. One could question; did these peoples consciously evolve beyond the human form? However, a more relevant question is; can we?

As we look for conscious existence elsewhere in time on this planet or elsewhere in the universe, we tend to look in terms of our own technologically based physical form. This rather self-centered mistake seems to be repeated over and over. Humankind once thought the earth was the center of the solar system and the universe. When we found out this was not the case we thought our solar system was the center of the universe. Then we found out differently. After realizing our solar system was simply on the edge of the Milky Way Galaxy, we thought our galaxy was the center of the universe. Again we found out differently. After finding out that our galaxy is not the center of the universe, but simply one of thousands of galaxies in our universe, we now think that our physical universe is all there is. We will find out differently.

We search for life as we know it on other heavenly bodies and if we find no embodied carbon originated life forms, we call the planet dead. I submit there are an unfathomable number of evolutions between the human being and the raw rhythms of the cosmos. These evolutions are simply unrecognizable to us in our present "frame" of mind. They could quite possibly even exist on or around our own planet. They are the "Wizard Energies" that will guide us beyond the human condition. Although they do sometimes *enter* the human form, they would not present themselves to us *as* a human form because of our tendency to war with any of our fellows who seriously challenge our present "station."

Many modern astronomers and physicists abhor war and press for us to search for other life in the universe to guide us in our own development. This is certainly better than war, but I suggest a search even more appropriate than a search for "others." I suggest a search for ourselves- our potential in the rhythms of the cosmos, for there is soon to be a coming of the wizards - and **we are the wizards.**

And for all my relatives:
    The animals
    The fish
    The birds
    The bugs
    The peoples
    The rocks
    The waters
    The dancing energies
And. . . the dust.

There are no secrets. . .
only stones unturned.

APPENDIX

It started with mittens
Mittens of light around my hands
Slippers of light around my feet
I could still pick things up
    but I could not feel them

Then the light grew up my arms
Up my legs
As this was happening
    it got stronger on my hands and feet
Had no control
Had trouble picking things up
Felt like my legs were stubs

Light keeps growing up my limbs
Around my body
By now my hands are gone
I cannot pick anything up
A mitten of light is all I have for a hand

Light has not begun around my head yet
It is around my neck
I am afraid I cannot walk
I am afraid
The fear is powerful
The light is gone.

Incidents

These incidents were entered in my Journal in late 1975.

July 1975

I run up the mountain every chance I get because it makes me feel good- real good. My mind often wanders while I run. Many thoughts go through it. Some keep going and some linger while I dwell on and develop them awhile. I was running back from the mountain on a the late summer afternoon. Thoughts were rolling through my mind but this time none of them were lingering. There seemed to be a growing span of time between the thoughts or activities of my mind. The movement was not continuous. There were vacant places in there. I recall having experienced this before to some extent, but this time the vacant places grew and grew until no activity was taking place in my head. No activity- vacant, void. I lost track with the physical act of running. I was not tired. I did not feel anything. As my body continued to run on "automatic", I rose away from it. I clearly remember looking down at the top of my head and my shoulders. I was floating above my body in total separation from it and the limits that prevailed.

July 1975

I had a dear friend, Steve, whose energy meshed with mine in a perfect way. There was mutual trust, respect and love between us. He had a dog named Rocky that he loved very much. I grew to know and love Rocky as he grew to know and love me. One day I was up in my pyramid and I turned around and clearly saw a ghost-like image of Rocky. I was not startled or afraid. I just registered the usual affectionate feeling I had when I saw him in the flesh. I received a message from him in my mind.. It was, "please tell Steve good-by." I knew I saw this ghost-like image and I knew I received the message but I didn't say anything to anybody immediately because I didn't think they would really believe it. The next day I was working with Steve and I asked him where Rocky was. Steve said Rocky had been gone for three days. I told Steve what had happened. Rocky was never seen again.

August 1975

It was the first night I was to sleep in the pyramid. I laid on the platform at the king's chamber level for awhile then fell asleep there on my back. I remember waking up to a high intensity, high frequency sound or ringing. The platform was tilting and floating. The walls of the pyramid were spinning. These affects were making me dizzy- something like being drunk only I had not been drinking. The tilting, spinning and ringing got so violent that I began to experience fear. I though I would get up and calm things down a bit. I tried to sit up but I couldn't even lift my head. It was as if I were held flat on my back by an intense gravity. I tried to lift my legs- my arms. I couldn't raise any part of my body. The tilting, spinning and ringing were getting more intense. I could not leave. I could not move. The fear was growing. As a last resort, I thought I could scream but when I opened my mouth, nothing came out. I could not make a sound. This brought the fear to an intense level such as I had never known. Suddenly, everything stopped. No tilting or spinning. No ringing. Shaking, I left the pyramid, not to return again that night. The fear had gotten so intense it closed my being to whatever was happening.

October 1975

It was a chilly autumn night in Taos. The rest of my household was asleep. I was playing my piano in the big room with a warm orange fire crackling and glowing. I was into the music and the fire. It all felt good. I often felt this way because I had been in a good place for quite some time. However, the happy feeling was slowly and subtly growing this night. It grew to the point of ecstasy. I could no longer play the piano. It was as if my body was receiving a strong current of some kind. I began walking around the room as this "feeling" of happiness kept getting stronger. I didn't see how I could stand it any stronger yet I felt it continue to build. I felt myself almost getting afraid. I could not believe that I was getting so happy that I was getting afraid. This was bizarre. It continued to grow as I walked around with my arms clutched into my chest wondering if I was actually going to be able to handle this electric ecstasy.

Up to this point, the experience seemed mostly physical and mental. Then I felt my spirit separate from my body and fill the room. There was an amazing feeling of knowing or awareness beyond words- beyond the earth.

November 1975

I was unable to sleep up on my pyramid platform. I came down to the big room and laid down on a couch. I was dozing, moving in and out of sleep. I think I was asleep when I became aware of a dull pressure on my lower forehead between my eyes. Then I began physically rising upward and outward feet first. I thought "I surely am asleep and this is a dream no matter how real it seems." I spoke, I felt around, and I looked up and around at the room. I was awake and floating at a 45 degree angle, feet up. I groped around in confusion and drifted back to the couch. This happened a few more times and each time I drifted back to the couch. I sat up and rubbed my eyes and felt my face in my hands. I was awake. I laid back down and waited. I began to feel the pressure on my forehead. My heart began pounding hard. I started floating out into the room again feet first. This time it was more powerful. I couldn't get back to the couch. I was headed toward the ceiling feet first. I felt like I was being pulled by the sky and was going to go right through the ceiling. Fear came. I was groping and clawing to get back to the couch. Before I even made it all the way back, I was mad at myself for fighting it. I promised myself I wouldn't fight it if it happened again. I won't fight it. I am ready.

The pyramid in Canon
where the journey began.

The pyramid on the mesa
where the journey continues.

One day in early 1976, I was in my studio working on an architectual drawing. The drawing was being done on a translucent piece of plastic which was taped over some other sketches and scribbles. These showed through the plastic as various foggy shapes and images. I let myself gaze into these images and they began to form this drawing. I traced the drawing and afterward wrote the following words about it:

"Be sensitive enough
        to feel how things are
Be wise enough to allow
        them to be that way
Beware of the two-headed beast."

At the time, I didn't quite know what this meant. I later came to realize these lines and this "drawing" were simply an early hint of what I was to find on my "journey."

Dated Excepts

In 1976 I began to feel that something was definitely going on within me which was not related to the "real world" around me. I kept notes of some of my feelings and thoughts during this time. Some of them were like memories from before I even existed and some were like insights that hinted that there doesn't even have to be an "I".

The following are a few excerpts from these notes:

4/9/76
And we, the volunteers, set sail in a ship with blue sails. We each planted a tree in a distant land. Then we became that tree so we could remain there until such time as our spirit could leave the tree and join the human species again to share what we once had on our homeland, which is no more.

4/12/76
I find that becoming the human is dangerous because it is so easy to forget what we really are, while we are in the human space. The cloak of humanity so often covers our "eyes." We should simply skate along the edge of humanity- close enough to participate in it but far enough away so as not to be consumed. Make the days you spend as a human give you the peace you need to stop being human- so nothing is there.

4/15/76
I used to meet with "those others" in my head to collaborate on a general direction and combine forces to proceed in the direction. I just went to meet with them last night and they were gone.

5/5/76
I am alone in my head. I no longer need "others" there. It seems there is very little I do need. I have taken the pledge of ignorance. This will expose my heart- a very vulnerable but powerful position in space.

5/7/76
I have suddenly realized the spirit that occupied this body (the body of Michael E. Reynolds 1945-1975) left- is gone. A new one has taken its place but it is different. The transformation (or switch) was over a period of "time." The old spirit left- the new one came. For a brief instant there was a void. I felt a white hot heat and now "I" (whatever that means) am different. The body looks the same but that which occupies the body is different. The mind remembers the old spirit that left. The mind experiences the new spirit that came. The first spirit of my body apparently laid the ground work for the second spirit. The old spirit appears to have *been contained* in the body and ego of Michael Reynolds. The new spirit appears to *contain* the body and ego of Michael Reynolds along with the rest of the universe.

225

Walking thru the hearts and minds of the
      people near my tree
Close enough to reach them with them never
      reaching me
I circled all their spaces and gathered all
      their gold
Then I gave it back the way it came
But I gave it back tenfold.

I watched them closing windows to keep out
      all the pain
That wasn't really there at all but its legend
      kept them sane
Sanity was the highway that took them thru their years
It kept them from ever touching me
It harbored all their fears.

No one really looked at me
No one really dared
They didn't see me laughing 'cause I wasn't
      really there
No one really looked at me
No one really dared
They didn't see me crying 'cause I wasn't
      really there
No one really looked at me
No one really dared
They didn't see me dying 'cause I wasn't
      really there.

7/13/76

I have been seeing blue dots before my eyes for about two or three weeks. They come twice or three times a day at least. I can't make them come or go by choice. They occur for only an instant.

7/18/76

The sky comes in pieces to me. I see it every day. I feel it too. I am it too. I am the sky. The sky comes in pieces to me. I see it every night. I feel it too. I am it too. I am the sky. The sun comes to take me. I want to go: I want to go. I will go. I will be. I will be. I will be the sun. Night covers. Night covers. I can penetrate night.

8/9/76

The island was full of thunder and activity. The twin women and I ran to the beach area. This area had been built over with tremendous platforms covering the sand beaches which were now below the water as the island was sinking slowly.

8/15/76

The blue dots are becoming blue splashes. They are also lasting longer than an instant. I feel something coming like I feel the winter is coming.

1/2/77

There is definitely a difference between "what I think" and "the critic of what I think", both of whom are "creatures" in my head. "What I think" is more spontaneous relative to reaction. "The critic of what I think" then reacts to that- sometimes in praise and sometimes in the form of a reprimand or question. "The critic of what I think" always has his act together, whereas the "what I think" often screws up. However, "the critic of what I think" is sometimes not at home. He flies is the sky a lot.

3/21/77

I am standing in the field. It is stormy. The sky is swirling with white clouds, grey clouds, blue, streaks of red. I am in an arena of universal energy. I am receiving something. It is an expanded feeling such as I have never known. How can I speak of it? How can I describe it? It must be shared.

Vision
Flashes of a sparkling kingdom
Castle-like cluster of buildings
Buildings seem to be made of jewels·
Glow in the night
Light up the fields around them.

Looking down at a little boy
This little boy is me.

The little boy is walking down a road
Road is white
Fields on either side are yellow
He comes to many places where the road forks into many other roads
He encounters people, all on foot
At each point where the road forks, the boy, without thinking
    about it at all, allows a magnetic feeling in his chest
      to pull him toward a specific branch of the fork. He then
      proceeds in that direction.
Sometimes many people follow him
Sometimes no one follows him
Sometimes people follow him- only much later.

Others always ponder over which way to go
He is always pulled without question. He keeps getting flashes of the sparkling
    kingdom
Each flash reveals a little more detail
The sparkling kingdom is the magnet pulling the boy.

After many incidents and many forks in the road the boy finds
    himself alone on a stronger, wider road with no forks.

More flashes of the sparkling kingdom.

A little girl appears from nowhere
She crosses his path
He is shocked
He feels the magnetic pull in his chest pulling him toward her
She seems to weave back and forth on and off of the road

He follows because they are still moving in the general
        direction of the sparkling kingdom
He is torn when they are not headed directly toward the
        sparkling kingdom
They coordinate and head directly toward the sparkling
        kingdom.

Flashes of gates that only admit two halves.

There are towering clusters of turrets nested in foliage
There are fields - Rolling, rolling fields lined and flanked
        with foliage
These fields lie to the northeast of the sparkling castles
I see the sun set behind the foliage to the west
I see the castles glow like jewels- like stars in the night
They light up the fields like silver light of a full moon.

I see a few days go by at the sparkling kingdom
I see people working in the fields
They don't talk
There is subtle music
The people beam
This is such a peaceful, high, glorious, rich earth scene
The people seem so in tune or at one with each other and with
        what they are doing.

I am in awe of this place.

The nights are revealed as well
The castles glow like stars
The people go into the castles at the day's end
Flashes of them all levitating and floating away
        in the sky.

There are also flashes of quiet, confident, subtle anticipation
        from the people as a whole
Looking down on the boy and girl, I see other people do appear
        briefly on the road but they aren't moving

The magnetic pull of the little girl was sharp and shallow at
    first- not nearly as strong and deep as the pull of the
    sparkling kingdom
This is what kept the boy from being torn in half
He seemed to always let the pull of the sparkling kingdom
    prevail.

The sparkling kingdom seemed to be pulling both beings as a unit
The magnetic pull between them ceased to act in resistance to
    the pull of the sparkling kingdom
The boy was no longer torn
He and the little girl become the same.

The road goes into a cloudy mist
The children disappear in the mist
There is still distance between them and the sparkling kingdom
    but they are on the road with no forks.

More flashes of the sparkling kingdom.

I see the children no more.

The vision is gone but the vivid memory of the sparkling kingdom
    remains.

I have been looking through this memory at the world before me
Its presence in my head is like a translucent screen through
    which everything appears softer and more beautiful
Often I focus more on this memory than the world it screens
It filters me from this world
It filters this world from me.

The sparkling kingdom could become the "real" world or the "real" world could become the sparkling kingdom.

It doesn't matter.

I know I am on my way to the sparkling kingdom, for this vision was an allegory of my life.

The sparkling kingdom has always pulled me but never so vivid and clear has it been illustrated to me,

Never have I actually seen it.

It has come,
It has gravitated your being
to a single spot.
It has formed a screen through
which your world is seen.

You feel things through it.
It is sometimes a barrier,
sometimes a womb.
It is outside you and you wish
it was inside.
You want it to *be* you.
You want to be it.

It takes a form now and then,
just to remind you of your
desire- your void.
You must become. . .

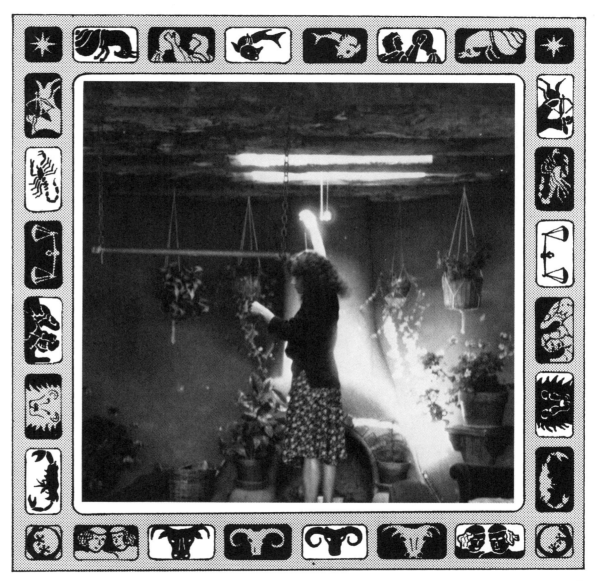

Love.

233